O9-BHK-802

Goldye Amadon

DAYS AND WAYS IN OLD BOSTON

Celebration on the Common of the Introduction of City Water 1848

DAYS AND WAYS IN OLD BOSTON

EDITED BY
WILLIAM S. ROSSITER

Drawings by Malcolm Fraser and Jacques Reich of the Art Staff of the Century Magazine, New York

BOSTON
R. H. STEARNS AND COMPANY
1915

THE RUMFORD PRESS
CONCORD, N. H.

PREFACE

Impressed with the interesting changes that had taken place in Boston and its business methods within the last two generations, we began some time since the preparation of a brief pamphlet calling attention to some of these changes which had occurred during the business life of Mr. R. H. Stearns, who founded this business in 1847 and died in 1909. It was our intention to distribute gratuitously this pamphlet (partly advertising and partly historical) among our customers. As the work progressed, however, we found so much of interest which had occurred in the year '47 and so much of Boston history which was connected with our present location, that the original plan of a small booklet was abandoned.

Moreover, competent judges advised us that the material thus collected was of more than passing importance—most of it indeed being of real historic value—which could not fail to interest a much wider circle of readers.

We therefore decided to eliminate the advertising matter (unless occasional reference in signed articles or illustrations showing some of the changes which have taken place at the historic corner where this business is now located could be so construed) and to print in permanent book form the material which had been collected. This volume is the result.

With this explanation we submit it to our friends with the hope that those who personally or through family ties are identified with old Boston will find it a welcome and permanent addition to the already considerable literature relating to the city, and that many others, without such associations, will derive both pleasure and inspiration from "Days and Ways in Old Boston."

R. H. Stearns and Company.

CONTENTS

ILLUSTRATIONS

Illustrations

Days and Ways in Old Boston

THE YEAR EIGHTEEN FORTY SEVEN

BY WILLIAM S. ROSSITER

War and politics conspired to make 1847 a year of much importance in the history of the United States. With the admission of Iowa December 28, 1846, the Union consisted of twenty-nine states and one territory. Part of Texas was in dispute, and the area which extends from the Rio Grande to the Oregon line and now includes the states of California, Nevada, Utah, New Mexico and Arizona and much of Colorado and Texas, comprising in all half a million square miles, was still a part of the Republic of Mexico. It was for the prize of this coveted territory that war was declared by the United States, and in 1847 the assault upon Mexican domain was carried to a successful conclusion.

NATIONAL EVENTS AND CONDITIONS

The peculiar importance in federal history of the year '47 did not arise from any deliberate purpose of Congress or the administration, but was an incidental result of the political exigencies of that period. This result was two fold:

The pro-slavery leaders determined to extend—at the expense of Mexico—the area from which to erect future slave holding states. This immediate object failed, but the southern leaders builded better than they realized. Victories in Mexico, culminating in 1847, added to the United States a section of the continent which was never available for slavery but which became almost immediately indispensable to the growth and destiny of the Republic.

The Mexican War, by the brilliant achievements of the American armies, aroused the pride and fired the martial spirit of the people, especially in the South. This successful war was a factor, probably of considerable importance, in determining the attitude of the southern states in the internal dissensions which soon led to civil war. In '47 the war news was a long succession of victories. In February General Taylor won the hard fought battle of Buena Vista. In March General Scott captured Vera Cruz. In April he won the battle of Cerro Gordo, while the crowning events of the war, the storming of Chapultepec and the capture of the City of Mexico came in September.

There are few twelve-month periods, therefore, in the century and a third elapsed since the Republic was organized, which have affected more powerfully its territory and its destiny.

In the year 1847 James K. Polk was President of the United States. The total population in that year according to an estimate made four years later by the superintendent of the Seventh Census, was 21,154,144. The inhabitants were still principally located in the original thirteen states. Many, however, were already settling in the rich agricultural areas which extended northward from Tennessee to the Lakes, and which benefited by the earliest immigration movement after the adoption of the constitution and the close of General Wayne's campaigns against the Indians. So strong was the tide of immigration that by 1854 not only were California and Wisconsin members of the Union, but Kansas, Utah, Minnesota, Nebraska, Oregon, Washington and New Mexico had advanced to the dignity of federal territories.

When the social conditions of that period are compared with those prevailing more than half a century later, the nation seems to have been conspicuous in '47 for plain living, and the preference shown by a homogeneous population for country life as compared with that in towns and cities. In 1850, indeed, three quarters of the population of the North Atlantic States dwelt in communities of less than 5,000 inhabitants and one quarter in large towns and cities, proportions which sixty-four years later are practically reversed.

New York contained about 475,000 inhabitants. Brooklyn, not yet a part of greater New York's vast population, was a modest independent city of approximately 75,000 souls, reached only by small ferry boats, after long periods of waiting. Chicago was a newly founded prairie town of about 20,000 inhabitants. Philadelphia, with its independent suburban towns, included about 300,000 people.

Boston in 1847

Boston was a small city,—as we now regard cities,— of 130,000 inhabitants, but this total did not include the quiet country population of Roxbury and Dorchester. Roxbury, however, by a vote of 837 to 129 had just resolved to become a city. Somerville had been set off from Charlestown but five years before, in 1842, and when made an independent town, it contained neither a post office, hotel, lawyer, clergyman nor physician. Brookline, now famous as a beautiful and wealthy suburb of 30,000 inhabitants, was a village of 2400 population.

Boston was not only small in population, but small in area. The broad streets and avenues which now stretch from the Public Garden, and are known as the Back Bay, sixty years ago were represented by open water or marsh. In fact, the Public Garden had but recently been reclaimed from a damp and undeveloped tract seemingly hopeless for any practical use. Where Beacon Street now descends the hill to stretch into the Back Bay district, was the famous "Mill Dam" connecting Boston with the narrow roadway that led to Brookline. This strip of land was wide enough to accommodate only a few buildings. Facing the Common on Beacon Street still lingered the John Hancock mansion, a famous old colonial home. Tremont and Boylston were residence streets, as were also Temple Place, Summer, Winter and Franklin Streets. Retail business—

THE ADAMS HOUSE IN 1847

and as we judge business today it was very decorous and deliberate—was confined principally to Washington Street, Scollay Square (including Tremont Row), Hanover, Court and State Streets, to which of course should be added the water front from which came in generous measure so much of Boston's material prosperity during the era of American commerce which culminated in the early fifties.

In 1847 the Revere House was completed and opened, and was regarded as easily the largest and finest hotel in New England. On June 29th, when President Polk visited Boston as the guest of the city, he was lodged at this new and sumptuous hotel. Other Boston hotels of that period were the Tremont House, Adams House, the American House and United States Hotel.

Aside from the State House, public buildings were few and of simple architecture when judged by the standards of later years. The Boston Post Office was located in the Merchants Exchange on State Street. It is difficult, indeed, to realize how business could be conducted at all with the limited mail service available in 1847. In that year there was one northern, one southern, and one eastern mail daily, three to Lowell, two each to Providence, Worcester, Springfield, Hartford and Albany. Other towns such as Haverhill, and Nashua, Manchester and Concord, N. H., averaged about two mails per day. The mail to England was received and forwarded twice each month. Boston and suburbs at this time sup-

TEMPLE PLACE IN 1860

The site of the first three buildings is now covered by the rear of the present ten story building facing Tremont St.

ported about 75 newspapers and periodicals of all kinds but their aggregate circulation was very limited.

During the year 1847 the Custom House was completed, and the corner stone of the Atheneum on Beacon Street was laid. On the latter occasion the address was delivered by Hon. Josiah Quincy. The year was made memorable in Boston by the breaking of ground in front of the old State House on Washington Street for pipes to carry water through the city. The law which made this public improvement possible had passed the legislature in April, 1846, and on being submitted to a popular vote in Boston was approved 4667 to 348. It is difficult now to understand how anyone could oppose the introduction of public water works. Later in the same year the ground was broken for an aqueduct at Long Pond, and Hon. John Quincy Adams took part in the ceremonies.

The revolution in methods of living which has occurred since 1847 is perhaps illustrated most strikingly by the change in transportation facilities. In the year 1847, Boston did not possess even one horse car line. Instead, the city and its suburbs were connected by various stage lines which furnished inadequate service to Roxbury, Cambridge, Charlestown, etc. One of these lines of primitive omnibuses ran at intervals of seven minutes from Charlestown to Scollay Square. Another line ran along Washington Street to "the Neck." Another line of omnibuses starting from Scollay

Square, connected Boston with Cambridge. Stages ran to Malden and other towns.

Railroads*

In 1847 there were eight railroad stations within the city limits of Boston. The Eastern Railroad which had been opened ten years before, was 71 miles in length, and subsequently was extended to Portland, a distance of 110 miles. The trains of

Eastern Railroad Station

this road were reached by crossing a ferry from Commercial Street to East Boston.

The Boston & Maine Railroad was 71 miles in length and was opened for travel in 1843. Another division, opened in 1845, passed through Reading, Malden and the suburban towns of that section. The Boston terminal, fronting on Haymarket Square, was a large brick building two

* The illustrations of railroad stations which appear in the following pages are reproductions of wood cuts published in 1852.

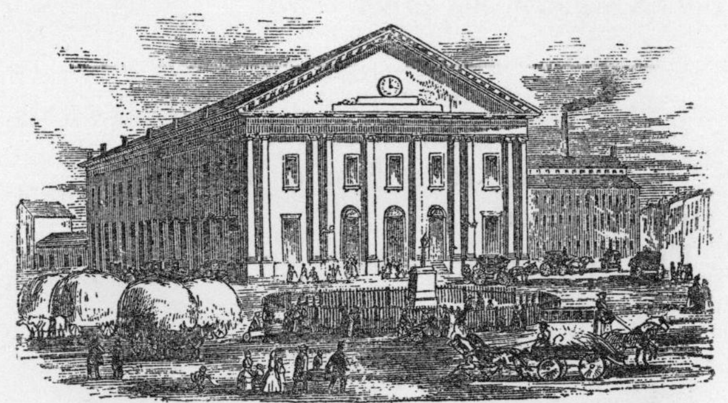

Boston and Maine Railroad Station

Fitchburg Railroad Station

stories in height, erected on the former bed of a canal. This was regarded as more centrally located than the other railroad stations. The ground floor of the building was utilized as a station, but the second floor, or loft, was rented by the railroad to a firm of merchants as a carpet wareroom.

This road was declared to be one of the most

Boston and Lowell Railroad Station

promising in New England, and it was said at that period that if any property of this kind could succeed, the Boston & Maine was destined to become very valuable.

The Boston & Lowell Railroad which had been opened in 1835 and subsequently extended, was said to be the most substantially constructed railway in Massachusetts. It was double tracked from Boston to Lowell, a distance of 26 miles; the tracks were laid on stone sleepers. A branch extended to Woburn. In 1847 the fare from

Back Bay Crossing of Boston and Providence and Boston and Worcester Railroads, 1836

Boston to Lowell was 65 cents and there were six trains daily, except Sunday, each way. The station in Boston, located at the foot of Lowell Street, was a plain brick building with no pretensions whatever to architectural elegance.

The Fitchburg Railroad, which had been opened for travel on March 5, 1845, extended 49 miles to Fitchburg and under lease a small branch was operated to Fresh Pond. The Boston terminal was located in Charlestown, but a few years later the building which now stands on Causeway Street was erected, and was regarded at the time as one of the most imposing stations in the United States. Between Boston and Fitchburg three trains were run daily each way (except Sunday). It is interesting to note that in '47 the entire rolling stock of the Fitchburg Railroad consisted of three six-wheeled locomotives, six eight-wheeled locomotives, 15 passenger cars, and freight cars which together were computed to equal 212 "four-wheeled cars."

The Boston and Worcester Railroad which connected the two cities, and covered a distance of 45 miles, had been opened for travel with a single track in 1835. The plain brick spacious station was located on the corner of Beach and Kneeland Streets. There were four passenger trains daily each way between Boston and Worcester. In addition, a freight train with passenger cars attached left Boston for Worcester at noon. This road was probably more largely patronized at that period than any of the others and by 1845 the income of the road was half a million dollars per annum. Worcester at this period had a population of approximately 10,000. It was the eastern terminus of the Western Railroad which ran from Worcester through Springfield to Albany, and was thus the junction for travelers passing between Boston and the Hudson River and Mohawk Valley regions.

Over the Boston and Worcester Railroad there

Boston and Worcester Railroad Station

were two trains daily between Boston and New York by way of Springfield, and in addition a boat train left at five p.m., via Worcester and Norwich.

The Boston and Providence Railroad had been in operation since the 4th of June, 1834. The station in Boston was a brick structure rather more pretentious than the other railway stations of that period. There was a two-train service

Boston and Providence Railroad Station

Old Colony Railroad Station

daily between these cities, one train in the morning and one in the afternoon in each direction. A "steamboat train" ran in the afternoon to Stonington. This road also operated four trains daily each way between Boston and Dedham, and two between Boston and Stoughton.

In 1847 the Old Colony Railroad had been in operation for more than a year. This road extended from Boston to Fall River and also from Braintree to Plymouth, with several short branch lines. The station was a three story brick structure at the corner of Kneeland and South Streets.

Transportation between the various railway stations in Boston or to different parts of the city was effected by the use of stages or "hacks." From the Boston and Lowell Station, for example, Cheney, Averill & Company operated an omnibus line to State Street. For this trip, without baggage, 6¼ cents was charged. Between the station and any part of the city proper, railroad carriages or omnibuses conveyed passengers for 12½ cents each.

Bostonians of the Period

In the year '47 the population of Boston was composed chiefly of the native stock. The city at that period was a distinctively New England community in which the citizens held to the conservatism and the comparatively simple habits of their ancestors.

The comment of Josiah P. Quincy writing in 1881 of the characteristics of Boston in 1800, applies almost equally well to the Boston of 1847:

"There were distinctions in Boston society which were the inheritance of old colonial and provincial relations.

"The population was chiefly of English descent. A type of manhood, ruddier and more robust than we are accustomed to meet, was to be seen in the streets. The citizens managed to be as comfortable at sixty degrees Fahrenheit as we are at seventy, and knew little of dyspepsia and those disordered nerve-centres which occasion their descendants so much trouble.

"Many of the peculiarities of Puritanism had been softened, and so much of the old severity as remained supported the moral standards which the God-fearing founders of the State had raised. A few men were accepted as the leaders of the community and lived under a wholesome conviction of responsibility for its good behavior. If the representatives of good society were in no sense cosmopolitan, their provincialism was honest, manly, and intelligent."

Thomas Wentworth Higginson

OTHER DAYS AND WAYS IN BOSTON AND CAMBRIDGE*

By Thomas Wentworth Higginson

In my youth the only public conveyance between Boston and Cambridge was Morse's hourly stage. The driver was a big, burly, red-faced man and the fare was twenty-five cents each way. We drove through the then open region, past Dana Hill, to the "Port," where we sometimes had to encounter, even on the stage-box, the open irreverence of the "Port chucks," a phrase applied to the boys of that locality, who kept up an antagonism now apparently extinct. Somehow, I do not know why, the Port delegation seemed to be larger and more pugnacious than the sons of college professors and college stewards. As we left the village of Old Cambridge, there were but few houses along the open road, until we came to the village at the Port. Leaving that behind us, we drove over more open roads, crossed the river by the old West Boston bridge, and came to the more thickly settled town of Boston.

But many people, in those days, walked back and forth, in spite of the celebrated Cambridge mud, which, I regret to say, still lingers in my native town. At the time of Charles Dickens' first visit to the States in 1842, one of my boyish play-

*Written in February, 1911.

mates, reporting a walk he had taken in Cambridge, said, "the soil clung to me like the women to Boz." However, it was very common for Boston and Cambridge ladies to walk back and forth to visit their friends and do their shopping. My mother often walked in and out of town. Indeed, from the shopping center, then located on Washington street, it was not too long a walk to Cambridge village or what is now called Harvard Square.

It was in the forties that I sometimes attended evening lectures in Boston. The walk between the two towns was to my boyish notions delightful, though it was a plunge into darkness. Here and there, in the distance, sputtered a dim oil lamp. But there was much more craft on the river, and I can remember being hailed, when crossing the bridge, and offered money to pilot a coasting schooner to Watertown. My old friend and schoolmate, James Russell Lowell, sometimes walked out with me from these lectures. On one of these walks with Lowell, I remember that we saw two men leaning over the bridge watching, what was not uncommon in those days, two seals playing in the water. As we approached we heard one of

JAMES RUSSELL LOWELL

the men say to the other, "Wal', now, do you 'spose them critters are common up this way! Be they, or *be* they?" "Wal'," said the other, "I dunno's they be, and I dunno *as* they be!" As we walked on, we speculated on the peculiarities of the New England rural dialect.

Before my birth my father had built a house, which is still standing, at the head of what was then called Professor's Row, but is now known as Kirkland Street. This led directly to East Cambridge which formed a separate village, and I remember once driving there with my father in the family chaise.

My elder brother, who was in college at the same time that Wendell Phillips was, used to say that Phillips was the only student of that period for whom the family carriage was habitually sent out to Cambridge on Saturday morning to bring him into Boston for Sunday.

On one end of Boston Common, near Park Street, there was once a playground where my cousins used to go and play ball; and when I went into Boston, I used often to go there and watch the game. They played with larger balls and larger bats than they do now and one of my cousins was a leader in all the games.

The East India trade still lingered in Boston, I remember, and Cambridge boys were sometimes sent to sea as a punishment or a cure for naughtiness.

WENDELL PHILLIPS

Groups of sailors sometimes strayed through Cambridge and there were aromatic smells about the Boston wharves.

My boyish friends were generally connected with college families; but I remember one boy alone with whom I was forbidden to associate. I am now inclined to doubt whether he had committed any greater offence than that of having gone to sea, and having brought back a little more freedom of language than was used by the other boys. I remember also that we used as a playground the large triangle of land which is now occupied by Memorial Hall, but then was used as an out-door gymnasium, constructed by the German professor, Dr. Follen. There were remains of the ladders and pits he had arranged and we used these pits to hold the collection of apples which we brought home as we came from school. A little later, as we grew older, we constructed a miniature post office in one of the gardens along the road where I lived, where we sent letters to one another. One of the largest boys, later the Rev. J. F. W. Ware, amused himself by writing satires about each of us and putting them into the post office where each could get his own.

North Cambridge, as yet, was not, though Porter's Tavern was a favorite place of resort; and we Old Cambridge boys watched with a pleased interest, not quite undemoralizing, the triumphant march of the "Harvard Washington Corps"—the college military company—to that hostelry for dinner on public days, and their less regular and decorous return. Near the Tavern was an open field where horse races took place.

At the time when I entered Harvard College, when I was nearly fourteen, my mother and sisters (my father having died) changed their abode to a house which my elder brother had built on the present Radcliffe College grounds, and which has only recently been taken down to make place for a more modern building. Harvard College then consisted of but few buildings as compared with the present time. There was no Hemenway Gymnasium and no Memorial Hall. We had what was called Commons, where a student, if he wished, could take his meals. These Commons were then in the lower part of University Hall. The customs of the students were quite different from their present habits. In the more boyish class of offences, such as breaking of windows, the making of bonfires, and hooting under the windows of unpopular instructors, there has been a change so great as to come near extinction. This is still more true of the robbing of hen-roosts and of market gardens, which would now be considered exceedingly bad form, but which was then a very common practice. I can recall members of my class, afterwards grave dignitaries, who used to go out in small parties on autumn evenings with large baskets, and bring them back laden with apples, pears, grapes and melons from the region now known as Belmont.

A cousin of mine from Virginia, who was in college with me, used to go out occasionally and rob a hen-roost and then he would show me how deliciously he could cook his booty by suspending it from a string before his open fire. The later practice of collecting signs and numbers from shops and dwelling-houses has, I trust, also gone out of fashion. At any rate, it is some years since I was obliged to give up having brass numbers on my house and substitute painted ones.

We went for our costumes to one Randage, a tailor, on Washington Street, Boston, whose store was a popular place for college boys to trade at, and our clothes were less sober then than now. The trousers had a strap of the same material attached to the bottom, so that this strap would fit under the shoe, the effect being that of a sort of gaiter. We would go for ice-cream to a well-known store on School Street, though I forget the name of the caterer. Theatres were not numerous, as they are now, but I remember the first time that I went to one. It was in the early forties, while I was in college and near the time when the elder Beecher (father of Henry Ward) boasted of having closed all such institutions in Boston. The play or opera, which I can vividly recall to this day, was "La Somnambula," and I shall never forget the remarkable actress who, in her sleep, walked down a supposed roof from a window and slid safely to the ground. My visit to this entertainment was mainly surreptitious, which enhanced its attractions, I suppose. I was taken very early to concerts in Boston, where I

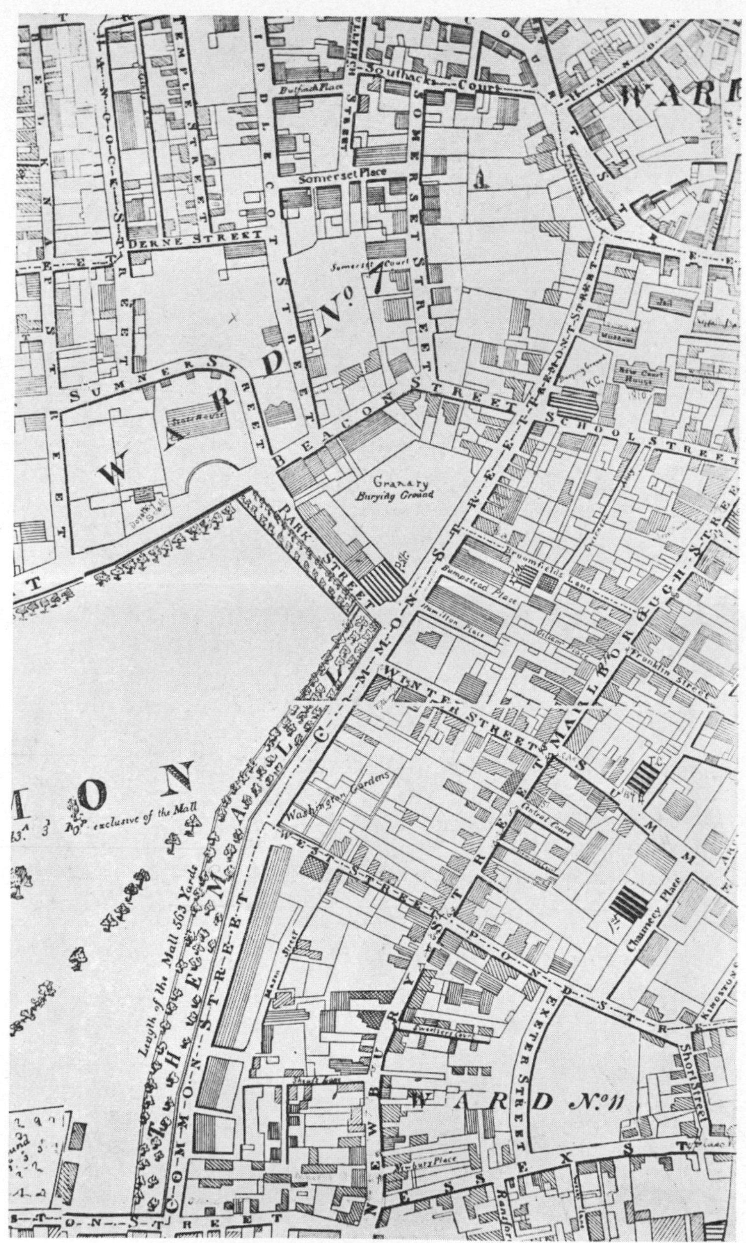

Map of Section of Boston, 1814

acted as escort to my stately aunt, Mrs. Francis Channing, who drove us in.

I find recorded, in the year 1845, that I was invited to hear the famous Ole Bull play at the house of Mr. James Lowell, who had asked a few people to meet him; but the great violinist did not come, and I wrote down at that time:—"The Lion from the North was to have walked out of Boston at 6 P. M. with John Hopper . . . but he appeared not, being lost in Cambridgeport lanes we supposed—I was sorry for he is said to be a charming person to know, so simple and natural and fresh."

In the same year I find the following entry in my letters: "At Cambridge we are in peace since the Texas petition (764 names, 13 ft. long, double column) went off." This petition was to oppose the admission of Texas to the Union.

In those days Christmas gifts were not the customary thing; but the making of presents was reserved until New Year's, although I find an account of celebrating Christmas by taking part in charades and dancing on that evening,—ending by joining Levi Thaxter (afterwards Celia Thaxter's husband) and giving a serenade to a certain Cambridge belle. I also find recorded that I broke down ignominiously in singing "Love wakes and weeps" and made an absurd exit, scrambling over fences.

This period was before the time of annual summer flittings, but there was a great deal of calling in the warm weather, especially at the house of

Samuel Perkins in Brookline. I remember when I lived in Brookline as tutor to his grandchildren—his wife being my aunt—how the family friends would drive out in the afternoon and be treated to fruit, cake, and the like, and visit the gardens, which were then quite unique. Daniel Webster came once, and it was my great good fortune to hand him some sugar for his cup of tea. Among the other guests came members of Brook Farm, some of whom wore peculiar costumes. Several times I drove one of my cousins out to fancy dress entertainments given by these social experimenters, where I must have seen Hawthorne; and George Curtis in his shirt-sleeves could be seen wiping dishes which the young ladies had washed.

Two years later I gave up this position of tutor which I had been filling, because I had decided that the best thing for me to do was to return to Cambridge and take up my studies again. I vividly remember my journey from Brookline to Cambridge. I procured a conveyance of some sort to bear my few earthly possessions,—boxes, trunks, and the like,—to my new quarters, but I walked most of the way in the mud, alongside of my belongings. In approaching the Charles River I came past what is now Soldiers' Field with its great stadium. Then, I looked out over open meadows and marshes which were overflowed at high tide; but how they are transformed now when they have become a playground for a great university! I also passed the farm of Emery Willard, whom we boys revered because he was reputed the strongest man in or near Cambridge. He kept the wood yard just across the Brighton Bridge, and I think I must have crossed over the same rickety bridge that spans the Charles at that point now. I read Irving's "Sketch Book" and "Bracebridge Hall" in those days and always identified Emery Willard with the "Ready Money Jack" of old England.

Beacon Street Mall about 1850

At this period the finest residences of Boston clustered around Beacon Hill. From Charles Street, this aristocratic region stretched up Beacon Street to the State House, and through some of the side streets. Many of the houses were separate, with gardens and grounds about them, and some of them were built in blocks. If I remember aright, Park Street had a row of houses built close together at that time. Beacon

Street was truthfully described by Holmes as "the sunny street that holds the sifted few," and young men and maidens in good society carried on their courtships while walking around the Common or down the long path or on the mill-dam. "Whom does Arabella walk with now?" was a question occasionally heard in careful circles of maiden aunts.

The Charles River with its accompanying marshes and low lands came up to Charles Street. Boats came and went freely along the river before all that region of marsh land had been filled in and transformed into what we call the Back Bay, a name which is sometimes puzzling to strangers who do not understand whether we are referring to land or water. Boston's first mayor, the father of Wendell Phillips, lived in this old locality around Beacon Hill, in a house which is still standing at the corner of Chestnut and Walnut Streets. I can remember when the summit of Beacon Hill ran up behind the State House and was about even with the base of the dome; but this hill was afterwards graded down about eighty feet, bringing it to its present level, and the material used for filling in the low lands.

The year 1847 was a notable year in Cambridge, for in that year, Professor Louis Agassiz came among us. Several characteristic anecdotes are told about

Louis Agassiz

this lovable and inspiring man and teacher. His wife called out to him in horror one evening, on opening her closet door, "Louis! there is a snake in my shoe!" and there came back the agonized cry, "Leezie, Leezie, where are the other five?"

It was in 1847, also, that Dr. O. W. Holmes, a native of whom Cambridge is always proud, be-

Oliver Wendell Holmes

came professor in the Harvard Medical School. Longfellow and Lowell were married and living in their respective Cambridge homes at this time. And "Sweet Auburn," a quiet rural spot, which in previous years had been a favorite and refreshing resort for Cambridge and Boston people, had been transformed into Mount Auburn cemetery.

At that time, according to my early schoolmate, Lowell, there were living old people in the region of Copp's Hill who thought that the United States had made a mistake in parting from Great Britain. The advent of new peoples with foreign speech and customs has swept aside many old traditions and transformed whole regions. But for us, who survive and who have seen the great transformations, there is still a lingering interest in the old landmarks and old memories which are but faintly recalled in these scattered reminiscences.

RECOLLECTIONS OF OLD BOSTON

From a Conversation with a Boston Lady of the Period

In my childhood I lived on Pearl Street. My home in those early days was a delightful old house with a large garden at the rear, which had been given to my father and mother at the time of their marriage. It fronted on Pearl Street, looking toward Oliver Street, but the garden extended back to Atkinson Street, a thoroughfare which I believe has long since vanished in the process of transforming that part of the city into the wholesale business district of Boston.

In the early forties Pearl Street was a delightful residence section, a region of fine old houses with a succession of beautiful gardens, for which, indeed, it was famous. I might almost say that my childhood was spent in a garden, for the custom of leaving the city during all or part of the summer months had not yet seized upon us. Although, to be sure, a few persons or families more restless than others, or envying friends who had travelled, sought the mountains or shore for a protracted absence of perhaps one week, these were rare exceptions, at least until after 1844, and so we were wont, as a matter of course, to remain at home the year around. Thus, in the summer months much of the recreation and enjoyment of the people of Boston were derived from the generous gardens which at that period were characteristic of nearly all of the better residence sections of the city.

In those days Pearl Street, strange as it may now seem, was a delightful place of residence in summer. It was near the water front and received the cooling breezes of the bay. The blue waters of the harbor were visible but a few steps from my home, and it was only necessary to cross High Street (which as a child I did with much trepidation) to quickly reach the shore.

There was considerable business transacted along the Boston wharves, at the period to which I refer, for the city at that period possessed an extensive foreign and coast trade, but there was little outward evidence of these in noise and bustle. Here and there appeared the tall masts and spars of brigs and schooners, and there were many white sails off shore, but steamboats had not yet come into general use for commercial purposes, and life along the water front was subdued, quiet and deliberate. The wharvcs and mansions of Portsmouth, N. H., as they appear today, seem to me to resemble in some respects the Boston of 1840.

My childhood in the old mansion on Pearl Street and life in the great garden are all delightful recollections. Many years later, while in Cheltenham, England, I called at the house of a friend residing in that city, and my surprise may be imagined when I suddenly observed as I stood upon the steps that the house was almost an exact counterpart of my old home upon Pearl Street in Boston.

The school which I attended was near our house; a plain little school house it was, without adornment, except for the hollyhocks which in this season blossomed beside it. Before long the encroachments of business began to be apparent, however, and though the old residents bitterly opposed the change, by the late forties warehouses intruded where gardens and old homes had been, and Pearl Street was speedily appropriated by the expanding business interests of the city.

I was born in Boston, but John Quincy Adams (who died in 1848) and my father's aunts resided in Quincy. I recollect clearly, even though I was a very small child, driving to the Quincy home for a Sunday visit to these relatives.

We lived in those days in very simple fashion. All dresses were made in the household; the stuffs were bought in the shops, which were located principally on Washington Street. I recollect that my mother made most of her purchases at Mr. Daniel's store. Sewing women came to the houses, and worked as seamstresses do today, but these women not only made the dresses for the women and girls of the household, but a tailoress came also, who made the coats and trousers for the boys. That was long before the era of ready made clothing for either sex. The dresses of that period, however, were generally very simple and required not more than a day and a half to make. Those for example which were worn every day were merely skirts "fulled on to the waist." One good dress of silk or satin or damask "for best" (which usually lasted for many years) and a very meagre wardrobe of gowns for daily use was all that the better class of women expected, or often possessed, in the Boston of the thirties and forties.

The furs we wore when we went visiting or sleighing, came, as I recall it, principally from France. I remember well a set of sable which as a young woman I possessed, and which I know came from that country. In extremely cold weather the men wore skin caps, of beaver and other furs, and coats of buffalo skins.

In my youth, and indeed until after the Civil War, nearly all our feminine needs were supplied by importations from abroad. Hosiery and dress goods other than calicoes and ginghams,—such goods, I mean, as poplins and silks—came from England, Ireland and France. Russian linens were especially fine, and as some of my family were engaged in foreign trade we were favored in securing goods of this kind. I recall that my mother had been presented at her marriage with a very beautiful set of household linen, made in Russia, in which was woven the American Eagle.

While the war was in progress much discussion occurred over the extensive use by Northern women of English and foreign goods, to which much opposition was shown, and it was said that we Americans should patronize home industries.

Bird's-eye View of Boston Common and Public Gardens, about 1850

One day I met on the Common James L. Little, who was the manager of the Lawrence Mills.

"If you want us to buy American dress goods," I said, "you must make stuffs suitable for our use. You cannot expect New England women to wear calicoes and prints in winter."

"That is true," he replied, "but we are too busy with the manufacture of prints to make any other kind of goods."

At that period our manufacturers were far behind the needs of the nation, and I presume in some classes of goods the same condition exists today.

At this distance even to the few who remain to personally recall it, the decade from 1840 to 1850 looks dim and remote. Senator Henry Cabot Lodge, in his recently published "Memories," summed up most effectively the change which was impending at that period:

"The year 1850 stood on the edge of a new time, but the old time was still visible from it, still indeed prevailed about it. The men and women of the elder time with the old feelings and habits were still numerous and for the most part quite unconscious that their world was slipping away from them. Hence, the atmosphere of our old stone house, and indeed of Boston itself was still an eighteenth century atmosphere, if we accept Sir Walter Besant's statement that the eighteenth century ended in 1837. But at all events it was entirely different from anything to be found today. Thus it happened that the year 1850 came at the dawn of the new time now plainly recognized, but the meaning and scope of which are as yet little understood, and the result of which can only be darkly guessed, because the past has but a dim light to throw on the untried paths ahead."

THE OLD BOSTON WATER FRONT*
1840–1850

By Frank H. Forbes

The newer and greater Boston that is to be dawns upon my vision. There are broad avenues and boulevards, terraces, parks, Charlesgates East and Charlesgates West, the Acropolis on Mars Hill reproduced on Beacon Hill. I can see huge and stately docks of stone and steel and brick on the North shore and on the South shore, and a fleet of ocean steam Leviathans, their sombre smokestacks outlining the horizon. But you will pardon an old man of three score and ten if he fondly turns back to another picture—inexpressibly dearer to him from old associations—the picture of the older, lesser Boston, with its crooked streets and narrow ways, the Common and the Frog Pond.

In one respect at least the older Boston surpassed the Boston of today. The pride of the city more than half a century ago was its water front stretching from north to south, indented and built up with spacious docks and wharves, with a forest of masts and spars, and a wealth of snowy canvas such as no other city in the Union could boast of.

In the forties Boston, so far as the extent and variety of its commerce was concerned, had no

* An unpublished address delivered before the Bostonian Society.

equal among the cities of the United States. There was no quarter of the civilized or uncivilized globe in which the enterprise, energy, and pluck of a Boston merchant and a Boston shipmaster did not find an entrance, or from which a wealth of commerce did not return. Cooper, the novelist, whose works were never regarded as the standard of truth, attempted to elevate New York at the expense of Boston; but facts tell another story. For more than twenty years, New York, Philadelphia, and Baltimore, as well as other business centers, depended largely upon Boston for the products of far-off countries. With many of the leading ports in Europe, Asia, Africa, South America, the West India Islands and the West Coast, Boston fairly had the monopoly of trade. The decade, from 1844 to 1854, witnessed the culmination of old Boston's prosperity as the leader in foreign trade.

The long stretch of improved water front, with its spacious wharves and docks, was the natural outcome of the commercial enterprise of the Boston of this period. In these the pride of the city was fully justified as well as in the fine warehouses which flanked them. No port from the capes of Florida to Casco Bay could boast of such wharves and docks. Before the filling of South Cove, the wharf and dock property represented fully one-fifth of the areas of old Boston. From what is now Dover Street bridge on the south, to Charlestown bridge on the north, was an unbroken water front available for wharf and dock purposes.

Old Boston Water Front about 1840

In this paper, however, I shall consider only such wharves as were in use for commercial purposes.

Upon the south, the first wharf, as I recall it, was Wales Wharf, leading off from Sea Street, with its quaint and venerable looking block of stone warehouses. This was the property of T. B. Wales & Co., then, and for years, one of the leading firms in Boston, having foreign connections, as well as large ship owners. This wharf was exclusively used by them.

Next was Russia Wharf, famous sixty years ago and owned by the Inches. This wharf was largely utilized for foreign trade. Liverpool and Fort Hill Wharves were next. The latter for years was the terminal point for vessels from the British Provinces. Next north was Arch Wharf. This was largely devoted to the West India trade and trade with the Provinces. It had some notable occupants in its day, such as Chas. Cole, Thos. Tremlett, Sheafe and Melledge.

Foster's Wharf, or Wharves, came next; there were two of them, north and south. I am not certain whether this property was incorporated or whether it was individual. This wharf, or rather these wharves, did the largest business under the occupancy of John H. Pearson & Co. They were large ship owners, and had an extensive foreign trade, particularly with Europe. Pearson had a long lease. He started a line of packets for Philadelphia, and later one for New Orleans. The latter line was composed of four ships, considered large at that period, built at Medford, expressly for packet service, the *Norfolk*, *Suffolk*, *Middlesex* and *Essex*. Neither line was successful. Pearson's lease terminated September 30, 1845, when he took a ten-years lease of Long Wharf. The last large ships that loaded there were the *Lochinvar* for New Orleans, and the *Michigan* for Mobile. Pearson did not make a fortune out of his lease, and the property had no particular distinction after that till it came into the possession of the present holders. Parties who knew Foster's wharf in 1844 would hardly recognize it as it is in 1894.

Rowe's Wharf has a very interesting history in the past, and is the only large wharf south of Union Street that has not been shorn of its proportions by the improvement consequent upon the laying out of Atlantic Avenue. The same old block of stores is still standing. It was a corporation when I first knew it, and probably for years before, the principal stockholders, as well as occupants, being the Richardsons and Cunninghams, large importers of fruit and other products from the south of Europe. The Cunninghams owned the one-time famous mail packet, the big *Harbinger*, running between Fayal and Boston. She was for years one of the features of the wharf. Rowe's Wharf did a large transient business, and its management was very popular with ship owners and ship masters. In 1848 Allen & Weltch took a long lease of this wharf, and transferred their lines of southern packets thence from Commercial Wharf. During their tenure the wharf did an immense and profitable business.

Next comes India Wharf, incorporated ninety years ago, the first in order going north of the grand old wharves of Boston. The East India business was largely represented by the occupants of the respective stores. As I remember them in the middle forties, there were the Austins, the Parkmans, the Lymans, and the Wigglesworths. The West India trade was represented by Benjamin Burgess & Sons, Philo S. Shelton, Atkins & Freeman, Homer & Sprague. Other foreign trades were represented by Boardman & Pope. Gardner & Co., John L. Gardner, Michael Simpson, Winsor Fay, R. B. Storer, N. F. Cunningham & Co., at one time the leading cotton merchants of Boston, were there for years. Not the least important occupant was old Sam Prince, the sail-maker. The wharfage income mainly accrued from the occupants of stores, but the wharf did a large transient business. Its annual income from all sources was not much less than $40,000.

The east side of India Street, from India Wharf, was practically a wharf for its entire length. Here were to be found regular packets between Boston and New York, Hartford, New London, Fairhaven, New Bedford and Nantucket. The berth adjoining India Wharf was generally occupied by large vessels belonging to John L. Gardner. The last of these that I remember was the brig *Pleiades*, and associated with her is the fact that she was sold at auction by Thos. W. Sears, the most accomplished auctioneer of his day in Boston; and this was the last sale he ever made. Another fact was that the *Pleiades* brought the last full cargo to Boston of pepper and cockroaches.

The Central Wharf and Wet Dock Co. was chartered in 1815. For a great many reasons Central Wharf was the most conspicuous and the most attractive of all the old Boston wharves. In the first place it had the largest continuous block of warehouses in the country. Its docks on the north and south side were continuous from India Street to the channel. Then it had the most varied commerce. Its merchants, and their ships and cargoes represented the trade and products of every quarter of the globe. Let me give the names of some of them—names now almost forgotten, but the very sound of which recalls the grand old era of Boston's commerce, when we did our own importing direct, and under the old flag—Perkins & Co., Mark Healey, Samuel C. Gray, Atkinson & Rollins, Whitney, Benj. Bangs, Bryant & Sturgis, Curtis & Stevenson, Eager, Kahler, Ray & Wheeler, the Foster's, Wm. F. Weld & Co., Wainwright & Tappan, Stanton, Fiske & Nichols, Joshua Blake, Barnard, Adams & Co., Wm. Worthington & Co., J. V. Bacon, Chandler, Howard & Co., Joseph Ballisted, Zacariah Jellison, Isaac Williamson, Herbert C. Hooper, Hill & Chamberlain, Fiske & Rice, H. &. R. Williams, Greeley & Guild. The Mediterranean trade was a prominent feature, and there was scarcely a day in the year that a vessel from one or more of the Mediterranean ports was not discharging. The Mediterranean fleet itself was conspicuous, comprising some of the finest clippers afloat, like the *Nautilus*, the *Martha Washington*, the *Emma Isadora*, and the *Griffin*.

The fruit season was a very interesting one, particularly to the boys on Wednesday and Saturday afternoons. Two-thirds of the length on the south side would be represented by alternate cargoes of oranges and lemons, figs and raisins. Central Wharf had two features, permanent the year around; huge piles of brimstone on the south side, and dyewoods on the north. Long Wharf had no particular features except the old salt stores, and the Hingham Station Packet, which was the landing place for old Commodore Sturgis, of revenue cutter fame, and the point of arrival and departure of the Custom House boarding officers, under old Kettel, and the news boat in command of Clive. Long Wharf was the terminal of lines of packets to Richmond and New York, and also of Alland & Troy's Philadelphia packets. That was in the days of Elihu Reed, Bangs, Rice & Thaxton, and Williams. Long Wharf was a favorite wharf for excursions and fishing parties, and from which the Mammoth Cod Association, one hundred strong, departed on their annual trips.

Under the management of old Elijah Loring it had a sort of sleepy existence. In 1845, however, it took a new start when John H. Pearson took a ten-years lease at $50,000 a year, and the United States erected the first block of bonded warehouses. The price paid was regarded as enormous, but Pearson was glad to renew the lease at its expiration, and during his fifteen-years tenure it was undoubtedly the best paying wharf property in Boston. Brimmer's T was a sort of leg set off from Long Wharf, but a noted wharf fifty and more years ago. In the early thirties Martin Brimmer erected a block of granite stores at the upper end. This block was occupied by Brimmer, Sprague, Soule & Co., Bramhall & Howe, and Sims and Eaton, with Lombard's sail loft overhead. Fifty years ago T Wharf was the noted fish wharf of Boston, with old Joe Locke of savory memory as its presiding genius. As you entered from Long Wharf, on the left was the largest establishment for packing dry fish in Boston. T Wharf was the center of a large trade with the British Provinces, and was the grand depot for grindstones. T Wharf is entitled to the credit of being the first wharf in Boston proper for the departure of ocean steamers. The first New York outside line, with the steamer *Ontario,* started from here; then the Philadelphia line with the *Kensington,* then the Halifax line, then the Metropolitan New York line, and then the Savannah line.

Commercial Street, from Long Wharf to Commercial Wharf, like India Street, was, on the east side, practically a wharf, and about the busiest locality in Boston. First there was City Wharf, the outcome of the genius of the older

Quincy, and a part of the original Market scheme. Then came Mercantile Wharf, the Baltimore, Philadelphia and Eastern packet piers. In 1832 City Wharf was leased for a period of twenty years to a syndicate of whom Wm. B. Reynolds was the head; later the lease was transferred to the Market Bank, who held it till the property was sold by the city in 1852. The stores were included in the lease. At one time I had from Josiah Stickney, late president of the bank, the amount of the lease and the net income above its earnings to the bank. At any rate it was immensely profitable for the bank. The sale of this property at public auction in Fanueil Hall, in 1852, was long remembered.

Mercantile Wharf and the adjoining piers, at the period of which I speak, was under lease to Horace Scudder & Co. The packet lines to New York, Philadelphia, Baltimore and Washington represented fully a hundred sail of vessels, barques, brigs and schooners, and a large portion of this fleet centered in this locality. The sailing days were Wednesdays and Saturdays, and on these days, especially during what was known as the packet season, Commercial Street was almost impassable. Commercial Street was practically the center of the grain trade, and there were always to be found fifteen or twenty vessels discharging their cargoes.

The entrance from the harbor to the upper north side of Long Wharf to City Wharf, Mercantile Wharf and the piers was between

Commercial and T Wharves, through a series of channels having very much the appearance of the canals of Venice. I think the entering and departing of this great fleet was one of the most exciting and interesting sights one ever beheld. This was before the days of steam tugs, when vessels of any description, from a ship to a sloop, used to beat in and out the harbor, and yet I have seen a whole fleet pass in through the dock between Commercial Wharf and T wharf, under full sail, and not let go a halyard till the berth at pier or wharf was reached.

Granite Wharf, or Commercial, was the first of the new North End structures, and far exceeded anything of the kind in Boston for its imposing massiveness. The old wharves were largely depleted of tenants to furnish occupants. The East India trade, the South American trade, Coast of Africa, Cape of Good Hope, Mediterranean, North of Europe, the West India Islands, and the Spanish main were represented by such firms as Bryant & Sturgis, Robert G. Shaw & Co., Daniel C. Bacon, Henry Oxhard, Enoch Train & Co., B. C. Clarke & Co., Wm. Perkins, Bates & Thaxton, Barnard, Adams & Co., Beccomb, Bartlett & Co., Hunnewell & Pierce, the Nickerson's, P. & S. Sprague, Ezra Weston, and so on. It was a high-toned wharf in those days, and if a fishing smack, or a lobster boat stuck its nose into the dock, it would have been fired out instanter. But it was some years later that the climax of wharf building was reached. A syndicate headed by Robert G. Shaw, John Brown, and Ammi C. Lombard, in the middle thirties, purchased the old Lewis, Spear and Hancock Wharves, and started the enterprise of building the new Lewis Wharf. It was at that period of wildest speculation throughout the country, and of course the enterprise was in advance of the times. The three parties I have named sunk nearly $50,000 each in the undertaking. But when completed, it stood forth as the crowning glory of commercial Boston. The docks and wharf were spacious, but far beyond these was the magnificent block of solid granite warehouses, that far surpassed anything of the kind in the United States, if not in the world. It soon attracted immigration from the older wharves; some of the wealthiest of Boston merchants took possession, bringing with them their large fleet of magnificent ships—Benjamin Bangs, then at the head of the Valparaiso trade, John Brown & Co., William Appleton & Co., then in the China and East India trade, Enoch Train & Co., who possibly contemplated his line of Liverpool packets, Sampson & Tappan, Lombard & Whitman, Isaac Winslow & Sons, Ammi C. Lombard & Co., Fairfield, Lincoln & Co., John L. Gardner.

Lewis Wharf reached its greatness during the decades 1840–1860. It was during the first decade that Train established his Liverpool line, composed of the finest ships that ever entered or sailed from the port of Boston. In the second decade Glidden & Williams started their famous line of clippers from San Francisco. Lewis Wharf was my first love—the Alma Mater from which I graduated, if not with high honors, with a full repertoire of interesting memories. No old Roman ever answered his hail with "*Civis Romanus sum*" more proudly than I did when I said "I am from Lewis Wharf."

North from Lewis were the old Eastern Railroad Wharf, Sargent's Wharf, May's Wharf or Union Wharf, Lincoln's Wharf, the old Marine railway, a distinctive feature of Boston's commerce, Battery Wharf, Constitution, Aspinwall's, Fiske's, Comer's, Ripley's, Grey's, Bartlett's, South and North Wharves, Clapp's Wharf, Brown's Wharf and Vinal's. All these wharves were important features in the commerce of Boston during the period to which I allude. The wharves gave character to the merchants, and the merchants gave character to the wharves.

Fifty years ago the average citizen, clerk, schoolboy and laborer could distinguish the merchant who did business on the wharf from any other class. He would come down in the morning, stop at the post office when it was in this building, obtain letters, then adjourn to Topliff's Reading Room in the basement. Later on, after the Exchange was built, go to the post office there, then to the News Room overhead, or to the Insurance Offices, and digest them. Then go down State Street in line, turning through Merchants Row and Chatham Row or Commercial Street, to the North-End wharves, or through Kilby, Broad and India Streets, to the South-End wharves, and at noon return by the same ways to high 'Change on State Street. The merchant's counting room and warehouse then were where his ships came in, and he personally supervised their loading and unloading. Fifty years ago a boy or clerk in an up-town store regarded it as a great privilege to be sent down to a wharf with a message, and he made the most of his time.

Our wharves then were in every truth water parks for the people, and contained no end of object lessons. On pleasant Sundays whole families resorted thither. On holidays or special gala occasions, they were immensely attractive; each vied with the other. Every description of craft, from a sloop to a full rigged ship, was rich in the display of canvas and bunting. It was a picture that at this date can be more easily imagined than described.

The "wharfingers" were men of no mean standing with the merchants and ship owners. They bore the same relative position to wharf corporations that today general managers bear to railroad corporations. Maccey of Rowe's, Brown of India, Blaney of Central, Loring of Long, Parker of City, Hersey of Commercial, Davison of Lewis, Pierce of Union, Homer of Battery, Elwell of Constitution, Wilder of Comey's, Redding of Brown's, were autocrats in their way, and from their decision there was no appeal.

The first break in our continuous water front

was in the thirties, when the dock between Central and Long was taken for the Custom House. The next, in the fifties, when City Wharf was sold, and when the Mercantile Wharf block and the State Street block were built. The last was in the sixties, when Atlantic Avenue was constructed. Then, and forever, departed the traditional glory of the old wharves of Boston.

Mrs. Julia Ward Howe

THE OLD ROSEWOOD DESK

By Maud Howe Elliott

There never was so beautiful, so wonderful a writing desk in the world as my mother's old rosewood secretary. It has four wide deep drawers in the lower part and one secret hiding-place. When you wish to write, you unlock and let down the front or "flap," faced with faded blue velvet—then you catch your breath—the sight of that marvellous interior, with its mysterious suggestions of romance, thrills you still after years of familiarity. First, there is the mirror at the back, where you can see your face, where she saw her face when it was young, without a line of care, her alabaster forehead, red-gold hair, eyes like beryls, just as you can see them today in Joseph Ames' portrait of her.

The desk, lined with pale yellow satinwood, has curving ornaments and small, neatly turned knobs of dark rosewood. It has fascinating secret drawers, that smell faintly of dried rose-leaves and lavender; in one of these I found a packet of time-stained papers. The first—a mere scrap of cream-colored parchment—set my heart beating, put my imagination to work, for it tells a story of old Boston. The writing is crabbed, the ink pale bronze, the spelling quaint:

July—

Mrs. Ward to E. Weld dett for horses and shay.

To Boston five times and horse ones to blue hill $7.

19th. Had the horse alone but did not use it (no charge)

22d	To Boston	1.50
24	To the neck	1.25
	5 chickens at 2 shillings apiece	1.66
	Ditto hen and chickens	5.50

Received payment in full

Ebenezer Weld.

"Nothing but an old bill," you say?

Yes, something more, the clew to a bit of family history. It tells us that in the pleasant summer weather of this year without a date my beautiful young grandmother, Mrs. Ward, came on a visit to her mother, Mrs. Cutler, who lived in the old colonial house in Jamaica Plain where Mr. George Wheelwright, Jr., now lives; that these two gay and lovely ladies drove to Boston, to the "neck," to "blue hill." I warrant they took whatever pleasure was "coming to them," in the same joyous spirit of thankfulness for life that marks those of their descendants, of whom we say "he" or "she" is a Cutler. Perhaps there was room in Ebenezer's shay for Mrs. Ward's little daughter Julia, to whom this rosewood desk belonged. If Ebenezer had been as exact as he was honest—I thank him now for not having charged for the horse the day it was "had" and not "used"—if he had dated his bill properly, we might fix the year of my mother's first visit to Boston, and determine whether or no the earliest of her many jaunts to the city was made with mother and grandmother in Ebenezer's shay. I am sure it was of the same genus as the One-Hoss Shay, painted yellow, lined with blue broadcloth, swung low and roomy between two vast wheels.

What visions this old bill evokes! The flush of those past pleasures whose price it records glows rosy through the dusky years. I am glad Grandmother Ward paid for those chickens, whether they were roasted, baked in a pie or added to Great-grandmother Cutler's hen-roost. Grandmother Cutler had to practice economy; it was only fitting that when her daughter, who had married a rich New York banker, came to stay she should "stand treat" for the outings and the poultry Ebenezer furnished.

As I lay the scrap of yellowed paper back in its shallow drawer, I look up at the portrait of Grandmother Ward over the chimneypiece, opposite the rosewood desk, and put the question we ask of each old portrait that we love:

"You liked your life?"

The brown eyes answer with their sweet half-distant smile:

"Yes, I liked it all!"

She died at twenty-seven, having borne seven children; six of them lived to grow up. The little Julia, though only five at the time of her mother's death, carried through life the happiest memories of her and remembered, oh! how faithfully, all her little lessons in behavior.

The next document in the bundle of old papers

is a letter from Grandmother Cutler, written in a clear strong hand on a double sheet, folded and sealed with a red wafer, addressed to the care of Samuel Ward, New York; it has neither envelope, express nor post mark. The letter was sent by a friend, for this was before the days of stamps, when postage was a heavy item.

Jamaica Plain, Tuesday afternoon.

My dear Daughter,

I send you this notice, by way of relieving your mind from your generally kind anxiety respecting me. I am tolerably well for me—but oh, the weather, the weather! When will it be settled again? I have been out of the house but once since the day I entered it. I have sent Mr. Ward, by the desire of the parson, Mr. M. L.'s address before the "Temperance Society," which I cannot but think through the interest he takes in it calculated to please him. I have read every word of it and am delighted with the performance. It is such a march of intellect—and bears down so forcibly and fully all before it—that I think it well calculated to be of extensive benefit to all mankind, and only wish there were copies sufficient to be distributed through the nation. Also as Mr. Ward will not probably bear the sound or sight of a Demijon in his house, I should be glad of the loan of one, as we have a fine parcel of "Mazard Cherries," to make it full of cherry bounce to send to McAllister and, indeed, I should like to send my friend Mr. Bullock another. I am going to send this down this evening by Mr. Chrismas to take tomorrow morning and hope my messenger will bring me a line in return from you. Love to all the dear chicks, believing me ever your affectionate and fond Mother.

Love to the Doc. He must read L's address as he loves genius.

Oh, Grandmother Cutler, Grandmother Cutler, dear daughter of Eve! At the moment you are sending a temperance tract to your sober son-in-law, Mr. Ward, in New York, you are plotting to get hold of one of his demijons to send "cherry bounce" to your jovial son-in-law McAllister of Savannah. Were you too that *rara avis*, the perfect mother-in-law? It looks like it! There's a good deal in heredity after all. Your most distinguished descendant, the granddaughter who kept your faded letter all her long life, was well loved by her sons-in-law too.

The phrase, so-and-so "is a Cutler," has become classic through use to four generations, so it must stand. From some of the letters in the old desk, however, it looks as if the term were a misnomer. That *joie de vivre*, that dancing of the blood it implies never came from the phlegmatic Dutch Cutlers, whose first ancestor in this country, John de Mesmekir of Holland, translated his name into English. No, that temperament, "the family champagne," came from Grandmother Cutler, in whose veins ran French Huguenot blood. She was Mitchell, a Virginian belle, niece of General Francis Marion "(the Swampfox of the Revolution)." General Washington once crossed a ballroom to speak with her, and Colonel Perkins—*the* Colonel Perkins of Boston —in talking of her to my mother said:

"I remember your grandmother Cutler as a fascinating widow with a lovely voice."

She was married at fourteen to Colonel Herne

and the tradition of her grief at parting with her dolls on her wedding morning still survives. Later she married Benjamin Cutler, Sheriff Cutler of Massachusetts, who died when she was still young, leaving her a great family of children and little else besides. Another tradition clings to her memory, vouched for by Colonel Perkins.

"At parties the Governor always gave his arm to Mrs. Cutler and took her in to supper, for though she was a widow and not rich, she was *très grande dame* and much respected."

After Grandmother Ward's death in 1824, grandfather often brought his little flock of motherless children to see their Grandmother Cutler. My mother always remembered a certain visit when they stayed at the Tremont House, at that time the most fashionable hotel in Boston. It was a massive building of grey granite, with vast stone columns in the Greco-American style, that stood where S. S. Pierce's shop now stands, at the corner of Tremont and Beacon Streets. The children's tutor, Mr. Joseph Cogswell, later the first librarian of the Astor Library, was of the party. The company at the Tremont House proved so gay, the table so rich, that Grandfather—a Puritan of the Puritans—fled from it in terror, taking his little people to the Mt. Washington House in South Boston. Dr. Cogswell and the young folks missed the goodies and the frivolities of the Tremont House, though they enjoyed the fine view and the splendid air of the Mt. Washington House, which stood on the high part of the peninsula that ends in City Point. At that time this promised to become the aristocratic quarter of Boston. Its natural advantages still make the Back Bay seem a poor place in comparison; even the Charles River Basin and the Fenway can not make up for that glorious outlook over Boston Bay and Harbor.

Another bill dated Paris, 1844, made out to Mme. Wowe for various embroidered muslin caps and dresses! Who says there is no romance in ancient receipts? If the rosewood desk held nothing but its old bills, I could construct from them its owner's intimate history. This French bill is for the layette of her first child, born in Rome in 1844; it is on crackly blue paper, written in a pointed French hand, and bears the revenue stamp for that year when Louis Philippe was on the throne of France. My father and mother were married in April, 1843, and after spending a year and a half in Europe they returned to Boston in the autumn of 1844. She found many changes in her adopted city.

The Mt. Washington House, a failure as a hotel, had now become the Perkins Institution for the Blind. My father, Dr. Samuel Gridley Howe, founder and director of the Institution, had fitted up a suite of rooms looking seaward. This now became my mother's first home in Boston. In those days the only public conveyance between South Boston and the city was an omnibus, that ran once in two hours. My mother adopted my father's mottoe, "Obstacles are things to overcome," and with characteristic energy set herself to overcome the obstacle of distance. She was determined to have for herself and for her family all that was best worth having in Boston, in spite of living at arm's length from it. For her the three great goods that city life could give were good preaching, good music, good society. I can just remember the old green omnibus; in winter the floor was covered with straw to keep the passengers' feet from freezing, in summer with woven hemp mats made by the pupils at our Institution. It was chiefly in pursuit of the aforesaid good things that my mother made her endless trips to Boston in the old green 'bus, "but though on pleasure she was bent she had a frugal mind," and she found time to do a deal of family shopping besides. It was a matter of pride to us that it was never necessary for her "to take a sample" with her. She could "match" the most delicate shade of silk, twist or trimming by memory perfectly. In her diary we find delightful little memoranda of things bought. At the foot of a page describing a lecture of Emerson's, tucked in, very small, on the last line, come the items:

> "Buttons for Flossie fourteen cents.
> White gloves two dollars.
> Trimming for Laura twenty-four cents.
> Rose for Julia twenty-five cents."

While she never to my knowledge copied these items into any separate book of expenses, they occur regularly; how they served her seems obscure. At the time when she was deeply absorbed in the study of German philosophy, page after page of the diary is devoted to Kant's Critique of Pure Reason or Hegel's Logik, then faithfully added at the bottom of the sheet: "two bananas for Julia and Flossie twelve cents." At that time we only had the fat red bananas; they were cheap at six cents apiece and often cost ten.

The fruit trade was then in the hands of the Irish. The old apple women still sat on the Common in their brave blue Kerry hoods and cloaks, their baskets of fruit and nuts beside them. In winter one sat at the head, the other at the foot of the "long coast"; in summer they moved to the shade of the elms on the Mall. They were powerful rivals to Marm Horn, whose neat little shop on Charles Street, between Chestnut and Mt. Vernon, provided the best pickled limes in Boston; her black molasses candy at a penny a stick remains unique in the history of confectionery. "The Rovers of Boston," the earliest association I ever joined, were divided in their views on the question, "Where can the weekly five-cent allowance best be spent?"

Governor Andrew's daughter stood out for Marm Horn's shop. I was loyal to a certain old apple woman. She was a terrific figure; when business was slack, she smoked a short black pipe; her voice was so gruff that I was secretly afraid of her. Her eyes were sharp and merry, however; her wrinkled cheeks were rosy as her apples, and there was something bold and free about the old dame that won my allegiance, though her fruit was usually dusty and sometimes stale. In the spring, when the weather was warm, the Rovers grew adventurous and hiked out to Mrs. Hankey's shop in Jamaica Plain, in search of the cocoanut cakes that made her name famous to many generations of girls and boys.

Mrs. Maloney was more enterprising and a good deal younger than the old apple women. She wheeled her fruit about the streets in a little cart and I remember my mother used to arrange her morning walk to meet Mrs. Maloney and buy the day's supply of oranges from her. But all this was much later, in the sixties, when we were living at 19 Boylston Place. At that time my mother herself did the marketing at the old Boylston market, that stood at the corner of Washington and Boylston Streets. It was a source of grief to her and to many housekeepers when this excellent market was done away with. While she was always too profoundly concerned with moral questions to think very deeply of material ones, there ran through the web of her character an odd little business thread, just to remind us that after all she was not only child of the muses but a banker's daughter. She never to my knowledge destroyed a receipt or a business paper; she drew her own cheques and kept her own bank account till the end of her life.

In the early days at South Boston, she always went on Sunday to hear Theodore Parker preach at the Melodeon. On one occasion the sermon was so long that she lost the omnibus that should have brought her home in time for Sunday dinner. As she entered the dining-room and found the family cross and hungry at dinner's delay (for no one would have thought of sitting down without her), she cried out, gaily forestalling all possible reproof:

"Let no one find fault, I have heard the greatest thing I shall ever hear!"

Parker had again "wielded the hammer of Thor," spoken in his most impassioned style of Daniel Webster and the rendition of the fugitive slave, Anthony Burns. It was a veritable handing round of the fiery cross; the ardent souls among the congregation went forth, each kindled according to his nature by the great preacher's zeal. In her "Reminiscences" my mother describes a meeting at the time of the attempted rendition of the fugitive slave, Shadrach.

"It was on this occasion," she writes, "that I first saw Colonel Higginson, who was then known as the Reverend Thomas Wentworth Higginson, pastor of a religious society in Worcester. The part assigned to him was

Theodore Parker

to read portions of the Scripture appropriate to the day. This he did with excellent effect."

Though the date of this meeting is not mentioned, it must have been in the early fifties. For more than half a century, my mother and Colonel Higginson met frequently on the platform at public gatherings. They became comrades in arms in the holy wars of Progress and Emancipation. They had many traits in common, the most vital perhaps being a profound sense of the greater importance of public matters as compared to private affairs. Both were of that small and gallant company who build the fortunes of the State. Both fought for the Union, the Colonel with the sword, my mother with the pen. The last meeting of the two old comrades was at my mother's ninety-first birthday reception. They sat side by side, sharing the honors due them as almost the last of the great army of leaders "God sent us for our need" in the troublous time of darkness and doubt.

> "Music went with me, fairy flute and viol,
> The utterance of fancies half expressed."

In these two lines of her poem, the "Voyage," my mother records her lifelong delight in music. In an "omnium gatherum" drawer of the old rosewood desk two "documents" lay side by side that at first seem to have little to do with each other; on second thoughts they prove to be links in the same long chain of pleasure. The first is a narrow slip of ancient paper cut from the journal of Auntie Francis, Grandmother Ward's sister, who brought up her motherless children.

"Julia began music with Mr. Boocock Tuesday, October 30th, 1831."

So this was the beginning of all that joy in music! No, for in 1831 she was twelve years old and by that time she was well advanced in music. Her first master was an irritable Frenchman, of whom she stood in such awe that she could remember little that he taught. Her musical education really began with Mr. Boocock, always gratefully remembered for having taught her to appreciate the works of Beethoven, Handel and Mozart. From the first she worked hard at her music and remained a good musician all her life. The "children's hour" always found her at the piano, singing for us the merry student songs her brother Sam brought home with him from the University of Heidelberg. As the children grew up and wandered abroad in search of new experiences, she was sometimes left alone in the precious twilight hour. How often I have come home at dusk to hear her dear voice ringing out true and clear in the cadences of the florid Italian operas of her youth, or throbbing with the romantic passionate melancholy of her own songs. Certain of these I could never hear without tears; one filled me with a strange, unbridled terror, a sonnet of Shakespeare's set to music of her own composition.

"Not a flower, not a flower sweet,
  On my black coffin let there be strewn;
Not a friend, not a friend greet
  My poor corpse, where my bones shall be thrown.

"A thousand thousand sighs to save,
  Lay me, O, where
Sad true love ne'er find my grave,
  To weep there."

On her catching sight of the terrified child, the melancholy song came to an end, the quick glancing hands struck the rollicking notes of Lannigan's Ball that set the little girl dancing and chased away the dread shadow of mortality.

The document found with the extract from Auntie Francis' journal is a member's ticket for the Handel and Haydn Society. One of the greatest pleasures of my mother's middle life was singing in the chorus of the Handel and Haydn. I remember her joy when my brother Henry Marion was old enough to join the society. The rehearsals were held on Sunday evening at half past seven; there used to be a great scramble to have supper early and get our two choristers off in time to their rehearsals at Bumstead Hall. They studied, under that splendid leonine old leader, Carl Zerrahn, the great choruses of the Messiah, Elijah, the Creation, Israel in Egypt, Judas Maccabaeus and Bach's Passion Music. My brother, who had a fine baritone voice, used to sing some of the arias to our mother's accompaniment. I can hear now the stirring notes of the great passage, "His voice is like a hammer that breaketh the rock," ring through the house, see her sitting at the old Chickering grand, her son standing at her side!

Mr. John Sullivan Dwight was one of the familiars at our house. My mother deeply sympathized with all his endless labor for the cause of good music in Boston. He was the chief moving force in the old Harvard Musical Concerts, forerunners of the grander but not more enjoyable Symphony Concerts of today. They were given in the Boston Music Hall on Thursday afternoons. We had our seats with Mr. Dwight in the front row of the lower balcony, where it was thought the music was heard best. The placing of the great organ in the Music Hall was a momentous event. I remember going to a concert while the work of putting up the organ was still incomplete, and the tremendous impression made by the colossi, the great brown carved wood caryatids that held up the façade of the organ, and the faces of the muses painted on the golden pipes. The other day at the ruined temple of Herakles, in Sicily, I was reminded of these wooden giants by the twin giants of stone that lie in fallen state upon the ground. The German wood-carver had seen Magna Grecia, drawn his inspiration from the unfailing source of Greek art.

One more treasure, kept these many years in the old writing desk! An ivory tessera with the head of Sophocles and the date of the performance of Antigone by the Saturday Morning Club. Well I remember her pleasure, her pride in the unique and beautiful production! The maidens who took the younger parts are matrons now, the young matrons are grandmothers; but to her they always remained her "Sat. Morn. Club" girls, the loving and loyal members of the Girls' Club she founded thirty-five years ago.

"What sense shall never know,
Soul shall remember;
Roses beneath the snow,
June in November."

ADVERTISING IN BOSTON, 1847–1914

By Robert Lincoln O'Brien,
Editor of the Boston Herald

If one were to pick up a newspaper of 64 years ago, the first thing with which one would be impressed would be the great preponderance of advertising over news matter. The *Boston Herald*, the *Boston Bee*, the *Boston Transcript* and the *Boston Courier* were all four-page newspapers in 1847. They were, contrary to the prevalent impression today, composed of about three-fourths advertising. Indeed, the newspaper then carried little else. A three-month old story of a Mexican War battle, a verbatim account of one of Charles Sumner's speeches, and some items of local interest, perhaps four or five columns in all, comprised the day's news. The second page of the paper was the news page; all of the first and last pages, and usually most of the third, were solid masses of small advertisements. The second and third pages were considered the most desirable, commanding double the price of the outside pages.

The better class of shops followed highly dignified and apparently well-defined forms. The *Bee* in 1847, for example, carried this advertisement: "Persons desirous of purchasing any goods at Auction Prices may do so by calling at

123 Court St., near Bowdoin Sq." This advertisement is typical in its bareness. The advertisers occupying the most space in those days, and in truth for nearly a half century afterwards, were the manufacturers of patent medicines. Their stamping-ground was usually on the first page, so that the first thing which greeted the reader's eye, on glancing at his newspaper, were long eulogies on the remarkable qualities of "Schenck's Pulmonic Syrup," "Buchan's Hungarian Balsam of Life," "Dr. Warren's Sarsaparilla, Tomato and Wild Cherry," and hordes of others of a similar nature.

Much advertising was inserted into the news columns in such form that the reader could not recognize it as such until he had read well into it. The *Boston Courier*, in 1847, besides an account of General Scott's advance on Vera Cruz, and in precisely the same kind of type, under the heading "Gourand's Lectures on Chemistry," set forth this information: "Another wonderful effect of chemical combination may thus be illustrated. Mix in a glass equal quantities of a saturated solution of Carbonate of Potash and a saturated solution of Muriate of Lime. Stir the mixture and it will instantly become a solid. When chemistry can produce such wonders, it is not at all surprising that Gourand's Italian Medicated Soap should be invested with the power of removing Pimples, Tan, Freckles, etc."

This attempt of advertisers to confuse the reader was aided by playing with the headings.

Evening Transcri

ORTH, PRINTERS TO THE STATE, NO 37 CONGRESS STREET, BOSTON, MASSACHUSETTS, AT FOUR DOLLARS PER AN

BOSTON, FRIDAY EVENING, NOVEMBER 12, 1847.

G-TAPES, 20, 40, 60, 80, and 100
, for sale at N. D. COTTON'S, 13
tc aug 25

AN'S KITCHEN FURNISHING
WAREROOMS,
ORNHILL, NEAR COURT STREET.
ap 7

OAM. Loam for re-potting Plants,
bulbs, can be furnished by AZELL
s Horticultural Seed Store, School st.
sept 28

D STATIONERY. School and
Books, Blank Books, Stationery and
ety, for sale at lowest cash prices, by
IPPLE, 35 Cornhill. tc oct 4

a lot of Land on Washington street
ner of Bedford street, containing 2347
of great improvement, and will give a
income on the investment. Apply to
State street. tc je 5

SHAWLS, from Auction—the
ns ever offered—a super quality, full
d colors, for $10; usual price $15.
t Row Silk and Shawl Store.
F. A. JONES, 5 Tremont Row.

MOND CEMENT. Just re-
supply of this *superior Cement*, for
ss and porcelain ware.
EPH BURNETT, Apothecary,
tc No 33 Tremont Row.

RY WATER LOAN. 6 PER
REST. City Scrip, bearing interest
ct pr annum, for a term of time not
may be had on application to
JAMES C. DUNN, City Treas'r.

BLE BELLS. JOHN E. AB
ashington street, has just received a
Polka Table Bells, of every style and
g new for Fountain Inks, with bell
at very low prices. tc oct 30

D THIS DAY, by MARTIN &
ashington st, four new songs from
orio, "Elijah;" also a beautiful duett
"Children pray this love to cherish."
oct 18

EOTYPE MINIATURES,
uted at J. J. P. DAVIS'S Gallery, No
oston. Large assortment of gold and
antly on hand. All materials used

BOSTON AND WORCESTER RAILROAD. CHANGE OF HOURS—TO BEGIN OCT 11TH.

ACCOMMODATION THROUGH TRAINS.

From Boston at 6 and 8 A. M. and 2¼ and 4 P. M.

A Freight Train, with Passenger Cars attached, will leave Boston for Worcester at 12½ M.

The first two trains will not stop to *land* passengers east of Needham; and the *last* train will not stop at all east of Framingham.

From Worcester at 7, 9¼ and 11.55 A. M, and 4 P. M.

The first train will *take up* no one east of Framingham.

Millbury Passengers will take the first and last trains each way.

NEW YORK TRAINS.

From Boston at 6 A. M, and 4 and 5 P. M; the first two by way of Springfield—the last via Norwich.

NEWTON SPECIAL TRAINS.

From Newton Lower Falls at 7 and 9¼ A. M; 5 & 8 P. M.
" Boston at 8½ A. M; 3½, 6 and 9 P. M.

SAXONVILLE TRAINS.

From Saxonville at 7½ A. M. and 1¼ P. M.
" Boston at 9½ A. M. and 4½ P. M.

All Baggage at its owner's risk.

oct 11 tc WM PARKER, Superintendent.

BOSTON AND LOWELL RAILROAD.

ARRANGEMENT OF PASSENGER TRAINS.

THE BOSTON AND LOWELL TRAINS

Leave Boston at 7, 9, and 11 A. M; 2½, 4½, and 6 P. M.
Leave Lowell at 7¼, 8½, and 11 A.M; 1½, 4½, & 5¾ P. M.

The Train from Boston at 11 A. M. will not stop to *leave* passengers at Medford or South Woburn.

The Trains from Lowell at 8½ A. M. and 1½ P. M. will not stop to *take* passengers at Medford or South Woburn.

The Trains from Boston at 4½ P. M. and from Lowell at 5¾ P. M. will not stop at East Cambridge at all, and will stop at no Way Station but Woburn Watering Place, except for passengers to or from the upper Railroad.

FARE, 65 CENTS.

THE WOBURN BRANCH TRAINS

Leave Woburn Centre 7½ & 9½ A. M; 1½ and 4¾ P. M.
Leave Boston at 8¼ and 11¾ A. M; 3 and 5½ P. M.

These Trains stop for Way Passengers at special stations, and new stopping places will be established when required. FARE, 25 CENTS.

MESSRS CHENEY, AVERILL & Co, will convey passengers between the Depot and State st, in Omnibuses, for 6¼ cents, (without baggage;) between the Depot and any part of the city proper, (except other depots,) in Railroad Coaches, for 12½ cts.

WALDO HIGGINSON,

HARNDEN'S EXPRESS, FOR BOSTON, NEW YORK, PROVIDENCE, PHILADELPHIA, AND THE SOUTH AND WEST.

PROPRIETORS:

BLAKE, COOLIDGE & WHEELER.

D. BRIGHAM Jr, } 8 Court street,
J. H. BLAKE, } Boston.
B. W. WHEELER, Union Buildings, Providence.
F. W. COOLIDGE, 6 Wall street, New York.
Office in Philadelphia, 43 South Third st. 6m oct 2

BOSTON AND PROVIDENCE RAILROAD. WINTER ARRANGEMENT. On and after Monday, Nov 1st, the Passenger Trains will run as follows:

STEAMBOAT TRAIN, VIA STONINGTON,

Leaves Boston every day, except Sunday, at 5 P. M.

ACCOMMODATION TRAINS

Leave Boston at 7½ A. M. and 3½ P. M.
Leave Providence at 8 A. M. and 3¾ P. M.

DEDHAM TRAINS

Leave Boston at 9 A. M, and 3, 5½ & 10½ P. M.
Leave Dedham at 8 & 10¼ A. M, 4½, & 9 P. M.

STOUGHTON TRAINS

Leave Boston at 11½ A. M. and 4½ P. M.
Leave Stoughton at 8 A. M. and 2½ P. M.

All Baggage is at the risk of the owners thereof.

nov 1 tc WM RAYMOND LEE, Sup't.

TIME ALTERED. FITCHBURG RAILROAD. On and after Wednesday, Oct 13th, 1847, Passenger Trains will run as follows:

Leave Charlestown for Fitchburg at 7 A. M, 1 P. M, and 4½ P. M. The 7 A. M. and 1 P. M. Trains connect with the Vermont & Massachusetts and Cheshire Railroads.

Leave Fitchburg for Charlestown at 7 and 10.45 A. M, and 4.40 P. M. The Down Trains from the Vermont & Massachusetts and Cheshire Railroads connect with the 10.45 A. M. and 4.40 P. M. Trains from Fitchburg.

WALTHAM TRAINS

Leave Charlestown for Waltham at 7 & 9.36 A. M, and 1, 2.15, 4½, and 5.55 P. M.

Leave Waltham for Charlestown at 7½, 9.3, & 11 A. M, and 11.33, 3.45, and 6.33 P. M.

LEXINGTON AND WEST CAMBRIDGE TRAINS

Leave Charlestown for Lexington at 10 A. M, and 2½ & 5¼ P. M.

Leave Lexington for Charlestown at 7½ & 11.15 A. M, and 4½ P. M.

FRESH POND, MOUNT AUBURN, AND WATERTOWN TRAINS,

Leave Charlestown for Watertown at 9 A. M, 12 M,

TEETH BRUSHES
TON'S, 13 Tremont Ro

AIR GOODS, of all de
from the manufacturers,
mont Row.

MOST APPROVED
DOW SHADE FIX
WOODWARD'S, 387 Washi

IVORY LEAVES F
for sale at N. D. COTTO
tc

ENGLISH DAIRY
ty, for sale by FRANC
tc

A LARGE LOT OF
SPARENT WINDOW
at very reduced prices, at BA
387 Washington st.

TO BE LET, Store No
Water st. Apply to HI
tc

FASHIONABLE F
assortment may be foun
corner of Avery st. Also m
pattern.

PERSPECTIVE.
and Sketching f om N
by a Teacher. For sale at
mont Row.

IN PRESS. The Song
torio, "ELIJAH," will b
MARTIN & BEALS, 184 W
Franklin st.

FALL SILKS. Th
cases rich Camelion, P
which we shall offer at unus
oct 4 tc F. A.

NEW STYLE
HOVEY, WILLIAMS
some very rich Chintz Pr
Co—newest patterns.

NEW GUITAR
day, several new and b
are those recently sung by J
MARTIN & BE
oct 22 tc

PAUL DE VERE

When some event was given special prominence in the news, the advertisers used the same heading. For example, on January 2, 1863, the *Boston Herald* printed Lincoln's Emancipation Proclamation under the word, in large type, "Proclamation." On the same and the adjacent page, a dozen advertisements appeared under "Proclamation" set up in precisely the same way.

The lack of classification of the newspaper advertisements in 1847 presents the amusing side of the subject. All the Boston dailies at that period had columns with headings "To Let," "Auctions," and "Board and Rooms." But regardless of fitness, the majority were lumped together, apparently in the order in which they had been received. On opening at random the files of an 1847 newspaper the following advertisements appear printed in order in the same column:—"To let in Temple St. a three story brick house"; "Bear's Oil at 12½ cents a bottle"; "S. L. Bedel would inform her friends that she will this day open at 154 Washington St. an elegant assortment of Ornaments for the head, beautiful Marabout Feathers, delicate Willows, and pretty Wreaths of Fruit and Flowers." This carelessness of classification was noticeable, although to a constantly less extent, for many years after 1847. In the *Herald* in 1863 a probate notice appears between a "Poultry Raffle at 18 Camden St.," and a sale of "Harness Leather."

The changes in the character of the advertising in the years subsequent to 1847 were few.

Newspapers at the end of the Civil War had approximately the same appearance as twenty years before. The only noteworthy change in this period was that the "wants ads" had become very well classified. About 1870 the leading news of the day began to be printed on the first page, and the more objectionable of the advertisements relegated to less conspicuous quarters.

By the middle seventies, the character of the advertising begins to change rapidly. Firm names which are now recognized as standard, such as R. H. Stearns & Co., Jordan Marsh & Co., and Shepard, Norwell & Co., begin to appear. Stores of this class were beginning to advertise on an increasingly large scale. Often they would use a half, or even a whole column, a small advertisement from 1914 standards, but a great increase over the six lines of three decades before. Coincident with this improvement in the quality of advertising in the Boston newspapers came a very marked diminution in the proportion of advertising to news matter. This tendency was due to the increase in the size of the newspapers.

About 1890, for the first time, advertisements began to occupy over a single column in width. The greatest advertisers were still the patent medicine manufacturers. Manufacturers of established lines of merchandise began to advertise extensively. It was not until well after 1890, however, that the big stores of Boston began to recognize the advantage of continual advertising. Once the movement was started, dry goods advertisements grew rapidly, both in frequency and size. In 1894 one of the Boston stores published in the *Herald* an advertisement a whole page wide and a half page deep for a week at a time. By the end of the century the department stores had grown to be the largest class of advertisers.

The greatest change of all in advertising, however, came with the turn of the century. Whole page advertisements appeared with frequency. Great improvement in illustrating methods made it possible to insert half-tone cuts in advertisements. Huge financial announcements came, in step with the consolidations of the first years of the new century. Industrial expansion was accompanied by advertising expansion. As stores doubled their size, they doubled their advertisements. And for all, advertising has proved, more truly than it ever was of speculation or competition, "the life of trade."

State House, from the Common, 1836

BOSTON AS A SHOPPING CITY

By Heloise E. Hersey

Civilized woman shops as naturally as she breathes. The Indian squaw grasps without discrimination whatever she can get, and delights in beads or blankets, hats or shoes with a complete disregard of the adaptability of each to her need. The first symptom of advance in the scale of living may be seen when she begins to choose and select, —to weigh advantage against price, to compare color and fabric, and to match both to her complexion and figure. The clerk on one side of the counter and the customer on the other write the history of society in the nations, whether the sale takes place in an Eastern bazaar with its dark-skinned merchant, its heavy perfumes, its long-drawn-out bargaining, and its final transfer of rich silk or precious stone, or whether it is made in the well-ordered, brilliantly lighted, highly organized American store, with its army of clerks trained to forestall the customer's desire, its mechanical devices to save the customer's time and strength, and its beguiling display to develop and to tempt the customer's taste.

The truth is that shopping is the vast barometer of social evolution. How far has the community climbed on the mountain path of progress? How many stages since barbarism was left behind?

How long before the nation shall instinctively choose the best,—sunshine and oxygen as against gloom and bad air,—durable and tasteful fabrics as against showy, shoddy ones? The market and the shop have the answers to these questions.

The methods of shopping mark the passage of the years in the history of a town as sharply as the rings on an oak tree mark its age. Each community develops its peculiar type of buying and selling for the needs of the individual and the family. In Constantinople the merchant carries his silks and velvets to the private apartments of his rich customer. In Paris, every lure to eye and touch is brought to bear to induce the customer to cross the threshold of the fascinating shop. One may travel over the face of the earth and observe in close detail the methods by which the seller of various cities makes traffic with the buyer, and works out the genius of his town and his time in his business and to his profit. If the shopman is a true Bostonian, for example, nine chances out of ten he knows his Robert Browning, or at least his wife is a member of the Browning Society; so quoting to himself Browning's immortal line, "Life's business being just the terrible choice," he sets about making that choice easy rather than difficult,—happy rather than tiresome. Boston will do it in its own way,—as different from the ways of other cities as her winding streets and her innocent Frog Pond are different from Philadelphia's prim parallels or London's tragic Serpentine.

From the point of view of the woman who buys, modern cities are divided into two great classes. Paris and New York are types of one class; London and Vienna and Moscow and Boston are types of the other. The Paris shop is made like the spider's web,—to catch the unwary fly of any race or color or plumpness. The window in the Rue de la Paix is dressed to attract the American or English woman, or the Parisian or Russian; and the trim demoiselle who serves the customer has an impersonal mastery of her business which impresses all alike, even if it is a bit chilling in its perfection. Not even your inability to speak her language melts her heart. She can sell you gloves and necklaces,—veritable imitation you may be sure, with a fine detachment, whether you are from Kansas or from Devonshire or from "the Provinces." So in New York—the Fifth Avenue clerk or the Seventh Avenue clerk is sublimely indifferent to your local habitation and your name. You may go to a famous confectioner ten times a year for five and twenty years, and the slender, black-robed woman who fills your modest order will write your address without a glimmer of a hint that she has ever heard it before. Whatever you are to her, you are not Yourself! Perhaps she condescends to recognize the Choicest of Her Choice,—but you need not aspire to join that charmed circle.

So much for New York and Paris. Boston and London are otherwise. The shopper in those cities expects and finds a personal recognition and a friendly interest which would wander about in Paris like a cat in a strange garret. The advantages of a huge, impersonal city are many; but the wise woman will not despise the delights of a small community,—half village, half city,—where name and taste and purse of everybody are known to everybody else. In fact, when these more intimate relations are once established and enjoyed, they are prized as one prizes the conveniences of home. It would be easy to enumerate a score of these personal satisfactions which come pleasantly to the surface of Boston shopping. For example, it is said that a certain man in a certain Boston shop knows the size of stocking worn by twice four hundred Boston women, any one of whom would feel it a definite personal slight for him to ask her the number of her hose or her address. A certain Boston florist hurries home from a short vacation on hearing of the death of a prominent man, "because it would be more trying for the family to order from a clerk the flowers for the funeral!" Not a woman experienced in Boston shopping but remembers with admiration the famous "Amanda,"—whose strong face and gaunt figure were "features" of the store of R. H. Stearns for a generation. She knew the pattern of ginghams and muslins that had graced the South Shore and the North Shore for forty years. Her memory of marriages and intermarriages and cousinships and even of family disagreements made her a perfect "Social Register" for the newcomer to Boston's inner circle.

One might easily make a collection of illustrations of the way in which customer and clerk in Boston take the personal relation as a matter of course, as much to be counted on as a business guaranty of goods or a prompt payment of bills. A customer at the small wares counter at one of the large stores heard one morning as she was selecting her needles and pins a queer noise beneath the counter. "What is that?" she asked; "it sounds like a small and lonesome kitten!" "It is a kitten," replied the clerk; "Miss Johnson brought it in an hour ago and asked me to take care of it for her until afternoon. It cries unless I hold it all the time!" So she nestled the tiny cat up to her neck, as if the care of it was a perfectly natural and agreeable part of the day's work!

This personal relation between buyer and seller is the very climax of the art of shopping as practiced by the dealers of London. Huge as is the business of the city, the old firms have never outgrown their early habit of regarding a patron as a valuable, personal asset. A stray American in the bookstore of Bernard Quaritch,—famous among the booksellers of the world,—was amused and amazed to hear an English customer suggest that the clerk should put a corner of Cheshire cheese into the budget of books which were to go to the "shooting box" in Scotland. The clerk seemed to regard the Cheshire cheese with the same friendly attention which he bestowed on the mixture of new novels and constitutional law which his customer ordered.

Emphasis on the personal relation between buyer and seller is nowhere more noticeable than in Boston, and nowhere in Boston more recognized by everybody concerned than at the sixty-seven-year-old establishment of R. H. Stearns and Company. At the close of the Christmas holidays of 1911 the firm issued a letter of cordial thanks to its employees for their hearty co-operation in the effort to make the best holiday business of their history. The phrases of the letter were full of real feeling, and one saw that customers and employees and partners were alike included in the general glow of satisfaction.

Next door to Stearns' famous corner stands old St. Paul's Church. It is in keeping with the traditions of the parish and its long career of helpfulness, and equally in keeping with the tradition of the firm for good neighborliness, that the church should recently have sent a letter to every person employed by its neighbor offering its help to each and every one of them in any way in which a church can serve. Intellectual and spiritual needs are recognized by both great institutions as being as imperative as the needs of the body. Church and store may work together. The doctor and the trained nurse make their rounds of the busy aisles of the shop, and priest and organist and choir boy and sexton give the welcome of religion to the worker who has also the claim of the Christian neighbor. By such means do gracious human activities grow and spread.

From one point of view modern life appears like a vast machine, the wheels of which are made of helpless human beings. Competition, the division of labor, the complete separation of the product from the person who produces it,—all these great economic facts which have come to pass since our grandmothers shopped seem to have conspired to take out of buying and selling all recognition of the person of buyer and seller and maker. But in the shop and in society there is working slowly and steadily another force, counteracting the tendency to make men and women into machines, and divorce their work from their welfare. This force goes by many names. One day it is called Socialism, another day it is called Human Brotherhood, another day it is called fantastically an "Uplift Movement." The names are only masquerades to conceal a shy reluctance on the part of men and women to speak the old-fashioned phrase of Christian Love. There are many evils in modern business life, and in modern society as related to business. But there is also a growing passion in the hearts of good folk to ameliorate those evils. There must be great factories where the workers are numbered by hundreds and are classed as "hands." But there are also employers to whom every pair of hands represents a living, toiling, hoping person. There are huge shops where the long procession of employees and customers moves through the aisles with no more personal recognition than as if they were so many mechanical toys, whole cities where the struggle for the newest kind of freedom has scarcely begun. In other cities it is well advanced,—the freedom of the community where modern civilization joins hands with brotherly love, and makes life worth living for all sorts and conditions of men.

Boston has never been so greedy of gain as some cities. She has never been so much in a hurry as others. Her shops have grown large and tempting, but they have never lost the air of those days when everybody in the town knew everybody else, and they all met at one or another of the historic "corners" in a sort of natural friendliness. Clerks and customers and owners and errand boys knew each other's names, and respected each other's work, and regarded each other's needs. Today the wisest of the merchants of Boston are taking that old friendliness and cherishing and invigorating it as a substantial part of their business. Recognition on both sides of the counter is counted as an asset by the firm and a privilege by the customer. In fact, it gives to Boston its distinctive character as a shopping city. "Do you know the name of every clerk in this store?" asked a New York woman of her Boston hostess in the midst of a morning of shopping. "No," was the reply; "but I wish I did, for most of them know my name and moreover they know what I like!" Perhaps this personal touch makes the stranger within our gates a little more strange than she likes to be, but to the Native Born it makes Boston the pleasantest shopping city in the world.

AN HISTORIC CORNER

TREMONT STREET AND TEMPLE PLACE

By Walter K. Watkins
Of the Bostonian Society

One of Nathaniel Hawthorne's stories of old New England is prefaced by a chapter which in effect describes the evolution from a wilderness to civilization: first the silence and solitude of the forest; then the Indian, stealing by, bent upon war or the chase; then the explorer, the hunter and the smoke of the settler's cabin and finally, after a couple of centuries of slow development, orderly towns and cities and dense population.

With much the same thought one may contemplate a number of historic localities in Boston, and shutting out the eager, insistent present—the tall buildings and hurrying throngs, the electric cars, automobiles and drays—step back into the twilight and the silence of the past, and picture the successive steps of settlement.

The present corner of Tremont Street and Temple Place possesses much historic interest. One must grope backward in time almost three hundred years to find this particular acre of ground unoccupied by men, and for most of that long period it has been the center of the city's activities and growth. By the middle of the 17th century it was a half cleared pasture, and here a little later was built the home of one of the first born in the colony. From this house we can imagine the outlook over a southward straggling path, rough and but half broken, along the Common, a mere bit of partially reclaimed marsh set aside as pasturage for the cows of the settlement while over all broods the silence of the unbroken, unexplored continent. Precarious in the extreme was the foothold of white settlements which only at Manhattan and a few other places broke the monotony of the wild shore line between Boston and Jamestown.

Both of these centers of European civilization, however, were more remote and shadowy to each other than Ispahan or Cape Town to the Americans of the twentieth century.

As the decades passed, the house at Tremont Street near what is now Temple Place, slowly became a venerable mansion about which clustered the home memories of birth and marriage and death. Owner succeeded owner, and unlike the usual American community in which all the local events, like incidents in a moving picture, are jumbled into an abnormally short space of time, the period of the colonial home at Tremont Street and Temple Place was long and deliberate, and stretched far into a second century. It suggests the age of Boston compared with most American cities, that our retrospect from the present to the days of the Revolution covers a shorter period than that other and earlier period spanned by the old House of Usher, from the date of its erection in 1684 to its final removal in 1830.

There are, indeed, few houses in the United States at the present time more venerable than was the Usher mansion when finally torn down. In the following pages the history of this mansion and the site upon which it stood is traced in some detail.

In the Days of the Settlement

In the month of June, 1630, Governor Winthrop's little fleet threaded its way between the green wooded islands of the harbor of Boston and passed the *Mary and John* anchored off Nantasket. The newcomers were saluted from Samuel Maverick's palisaded house at Winnisimmet, and the Spragues welcomed them to the shores of the Mystic. On the south slope of the west hill of that crown of peaks which gave the name of Trimount to the settlement, dwelt William Blackstone in a thatched house flanked by a ruder garden.

After a score of years let us ascend the Beacon Hill, the center of the crown, and view the growth of the town of Boston.

Houses fringe the water front from Merry's Point at the North End to Fort Point at Fort Hill. They are thickly clustered about the Town Cove, which indented the shore to the present Adams Square. On the High Street to the water (now State Street) were the homes of the town fathers and on the High or Fore Street to Roxbury, now Washington Street, were the houses of prosperous tradesmen, their shops on the ground floor and their dwellings above, as is the custom still in Old England. These houses on the highway to Roxbury were each surrounded by the goodly part of an acre of garden with orchards in the rear. On the west side of this street, south of Winter Street, these orchards extended back to a fringe of pastures which skirted the "Common land" on the east. One of these pastures, an acre and a half, was between the site of St. Paul's Church and West Street. In it grazed the cattle of Henry Webb, a prosperous merchant, who dwelt opposite the Market Place, now the Old State House site. In poor grazing seasons a pasture which he owned on Fort Hill also gave forage to his cattle. His warehouse faced the Town Dock and his vessels unloading at his wharf lay where a century later Faneuil Hall was erected.

Back of his house, which stood on the corner of what is now State and Devonshire Streets, lived William Parsons, a carpenter and "sley-maker." Parsons was destined to help make history as one of the "Fifth Monarchy" men who ran a bloody riot in London Streets in 1661, but he did not meet the fate of his leader that other Boston man, Thomas Venner, who was hung, drawn and quartered, for Parsons slipped away in the crowd and fled back to New England. There, when well advanced in years, and known as "Old Will Parsons," he sold drinks in front of his house. It was to him that Webb sold his pasture but by 1646 Parsons had disposed of the land to Richard Carter, also a carpenter.

Carter lived not far away on the High Street to Roxbury, south of West Street, and on the site of what became later the "Lamb Tavern" and is now covered by the Adams House. His wife was evidently an advanced woman, or suffragette of the period, as she was admonished twice for seditious words. She survived her husband and married John Hunt of Charlestown. A daughter, Mary, for a second husband espoused a neighbor, Joseph Cowell, who lived on the south corner of West and Washington Streets. From his residence there West Street was early known as Cowell's Lane, and down the lane to the pasture he led the horses that he rode as messenger for the Colony to Hartford and New York.

In 1680 Mrs. Hunt and her daughter Mrs. Cowell, sold the pasture to Hezekiah Usher Junior. Hezekiah Usher, Senior, was the first bookseller of the colony. He lived on the north side of the Market Place and his warehouse in the rear faced the Town Dock. He died in 1676, leaving a goodly fortune and two sons to quarrel over it and evoke the aid of the law. Six months after his father's death Hezekiah Usher married Bridget, the widow of Dr. Leonard Hoar, President of Harvard College. Mrs. Usher's parents were Lord John Lisle, who was assassinated at Lausanne, Switzerland, in 1664, and Lady Alicia Lisle, beheaded at Winchester, England, in 1685. After a few years of married life, spent in the house he erected in 1684 in Carter's pasture, Usher developed such eccentricities that in 1687 Mrs.

Mansion Erected by Hezekiah Usher in 1684 on What is now the Corner of Tremont Street and Temple Place

Usher and her daughter, by her previous marriage, left Usher and sailed for England, the husband weeping bitterly.

Left alone, Usher was discontented and unhappy. In May, 1688, he leased his house to John West, secretary to Andros, the new governor of the colony. West had come to New York in 1678, became the town clerk and married the daughter of Thomas Rudyard, lieutenant governor of New Jersey. It was shortly after the arrival of West in Boston, in June, 1688, at the Usher house, that Andros had his stormy interview with Judge Sewall in regard to occupying the Old South Meeting House as a place of worship. Soon afterward Andros was confined in the Fort and West in the common prison, until they were sent back to England in February, 1689. Two years later, in 1691, West died in his lodgings in St. Martins, Ludgate parish, London. In a few years his widow again married, having obtained for West's services grants of lands at Barnegat and elsewhere in New Jersey. For a third husband she married Andrew Hamilton, speaker of the Pennsylvania Assembly. Her daughter married Chief Justice Allen and her grand-daughter was the wife of the son of Richard Penn, last proprietary governor of Pennsylvania.

When West vacated the Usher house it was rented to Waitstill Winthrop, grandson of the first governor. Winthrop was a prominent citizen of Boston, a Judge, councillor, and of high rank in the militia. In 1692 his house was brilliant

Waitstill Winthrop

with illumination when the province government began under the new charter. In September of the same year, it was the scene of stately festivities when his daughter, Anne, was married to Major John Richards. Here also Winthrop conferred with his townsmen in regard to that epidemic of witchcraft which convulsed New England in 1692. The owner of the house, Hezekiah Usher, with his many eccentricities, did not escape suspicion, and was accused by Susanna Sheldon of Salem. She declared that he stuck pins into her, but his brother and Winthrop prevented prosecution.

In the winter of 1696–7 while Usher was on a journey, he fell from his horse in the town of Malden and was taken to the tavern of Isaac Hill in an injured condition, where he became worse, mentally and physically. His brother was made his guardian and in April, 1697, he was removed to Lynn, where he died in July. Usher's body was brought to Boston and placed in his father's tomb in the King's Chapel Burial Ground. Passers-by can readily read the inscription on the tomb located next the "old Registry Building." His will clearly shows his disordered mind and in it he bitterly denounces his wife.

Mrs. Usher had attempted to obtain the family home before her husband's death, upon the authority of a deed of gift given at the time of marriage. An effort to eject Winthrop the tenant was unsuccessful, but upon Usher's death Mr. Winthrop moved; but suits were brought

THE USHER TOMB IN KING'S CHAPEL BURYING GROUND

by Judge Sewall as Mrs. Usher's attorney against the executor and tenant for possession. Mrs. Usher was successful in the lower and higher courts and the case was appealed by Usher's executor to the Privy Council in England. Their confirmation of Mrs. Usher's right was received in 1700 and she came into possession of the house. Judge Sewall presented to his client a cord of wood from Muddy River (as Brookline was then called), to start housekeeping. Mrs. Usher held possession of the house till 1714. Her death occurred in 1725.

In the Days of the Province

In 1714 Mrs. Usher sold the mansion to Francis Wainwright of Ipswich. His father, Colonel John, left him considerable wealth. He also inherited through his mother, a niece of Rev. John Norton, lands in Ipswich granted that minister. Coming to Boston, Wainwright married a daughter of Governor Joseph Dudley. His business ventures, however, were unsuccessful, and he mortgaged the Usher house together with other properties. The mortgage upon the former was not paid; he was sued in 1720 for possession, and transferred the Usher house to Deacon Jonathan Williams, a wine cooper.

Wainwright was never prominent in town affairs in Boston. He did hold the office of constable, but his only official act, if it could be so termed, was a failure to warn a town meeting in 1713, and for this he was censured with his fellow constables, equally guilty. He died in 1722 and his widow married again, as was the custom in those days.

The new proprietor of the Usher house, Deacon Williams, had married, as his second wife, Rebecca, the widow of James Townsend, wine merchant. With her he took her worldly goods, which were on sale in the wine shop of her late husband on Cornhill (now Washington Street) and known as the sign of "The Black Boy and Butt."

Williams' residence was in Savage's Court off Cornhill, which later took the name of Williams Court. This name it still retains with its alias of Pie Alley. Williams also owned a block of three houses on Portland Street, then Cold Lane.

The mansion house of Usher now secured a tenant of more note in the person of Rev. Roger Price of King's Chapel. Of an ancient Welsh family which had settled in Buckinghamshire, he was educated for the church. After his course at Oxford he went as a chaplain on the coast of Guinea. There he was captured by pirates, and on his release went to St. Anne's, Jamaica, as chaplain. Both experiences contributed to ill health and he returned to England. His health not improving, he accepted a position in Boston, arriving in 1729. He first lodged with Peter Feust or Feuart, a Dutchman, on Marlboro now Washington Street. His relations with Rev. Henry Harris and Rev. Thomas Harward, successively the rectors of King's Chapel, were not the most pleasant. At last, in 1733, he decided

Wedding Gown (1735) of Mistress Roger Price

to return to England and even engaged passage. Contrary winds, however, delayed departure, and while waiting to sail he attended Trinity Church and saw Miss Elizabeth Bull. All thoughts of departure were driven from his mind; he secured presentation to the young lady and assiduously paid her court. Miss Bull was regarded as one of the beauties of that period. She was the grandchild of old Sergeant Bull, who kept the "Bull Tavern" by the waterside at the foot of Summer Street, the "Seven Star Lane" of those days. After a lengthy courtship they were married in 1735 and went to reside in the Usher house. We can imagine the dainty bride clothed in the finely embroidered wedding gown, which with the linen of her young children is still preserved and is now in the Collections of the Bostonian Society.

Meanwhile, Deacon Williams was gathered to his fathers, and once more the spirit of litigation, seemingly framed into the very timbers of the house by its first owner, again appeared. Controversy over the partition of the deacon's estate brought the matter before the Superior Court of Judicature and on an appeal to the Governor and Council, the property was sold in 1742 to Mr. Stephen Greenleaf. In a few years Mr. Roger Price and family removed to Hopkinton, where he established a church and Mr. Greenleaf became the occupant of the mansion as well as its owner.

Sheriff Stephen Greenleaf

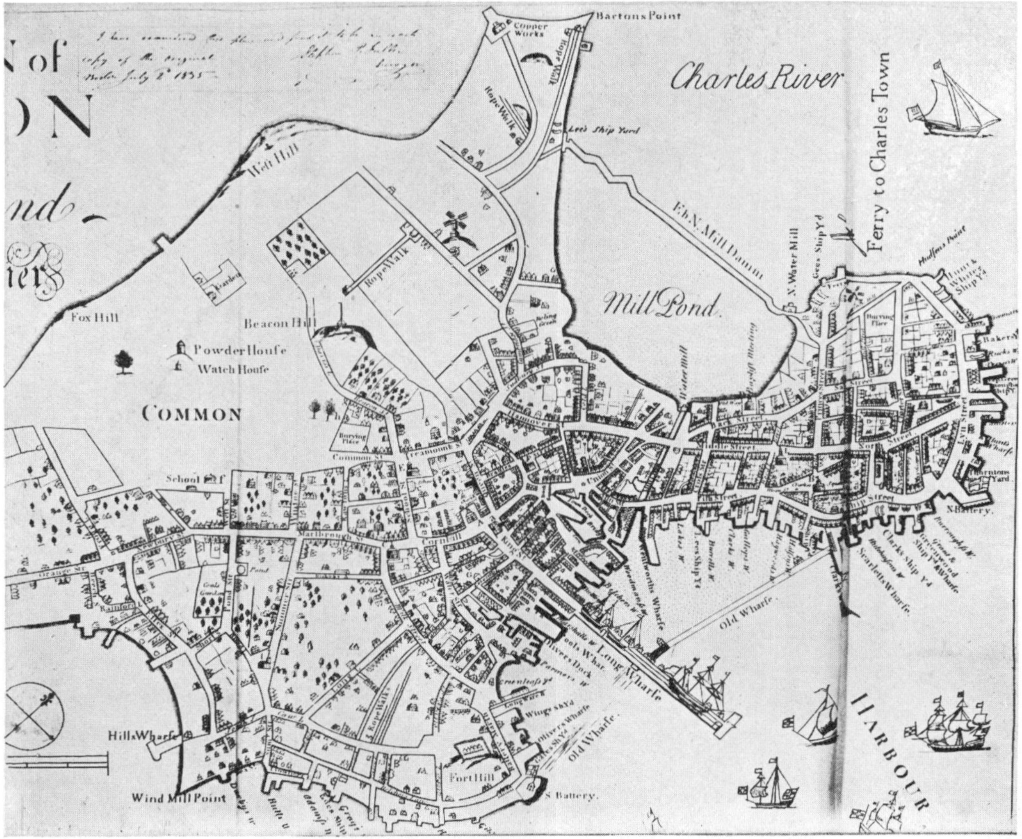

Map of Boston. 1722

The Revolutionary Period

Stephen Greenleaf was born in Newbury in 1704. Inheriting wealth, he married in 1731 and came to reside in Boston. In 1757 he was appointed sheriff of Suffolk County. In August following Greenleaf's appointment, Thomas Pownall arrived as governor of the province and in the next year Thomas Hutchinson became lieutenant-governor. In September (1758), General Lord Amherst arrived in Boston and his troops encamped on the Common near the old Usher mansion on their way to Lake George. The same year saw Pownall depart for South Carolina, and the sheriff early in August headed a detachment of the governor's troop of guards and rode to Wrentham to welcome the new governor, Francis Bernard, and act as his escort to Boston.

In December, 1758, Greenleaf, from the balcony of the Town House, proclaimed the new King, George the Third, and a few days later assisted in the funeral ceremonies for the late King.

Soon began the oppression of the colony through acts of the crown officers, more especially those of the revenue and customs. Because of his official position Greenleaf became an actor in the scenes and incidents resulting from the opposition of Otis and his friends to the writs of assistance. Upon an August day in 1765 word was brought him that Bute and Oliver (the stamp officer) were hanging in effigy from the Liberty

The John Hancock Mansion
(From an old print published in 1852)

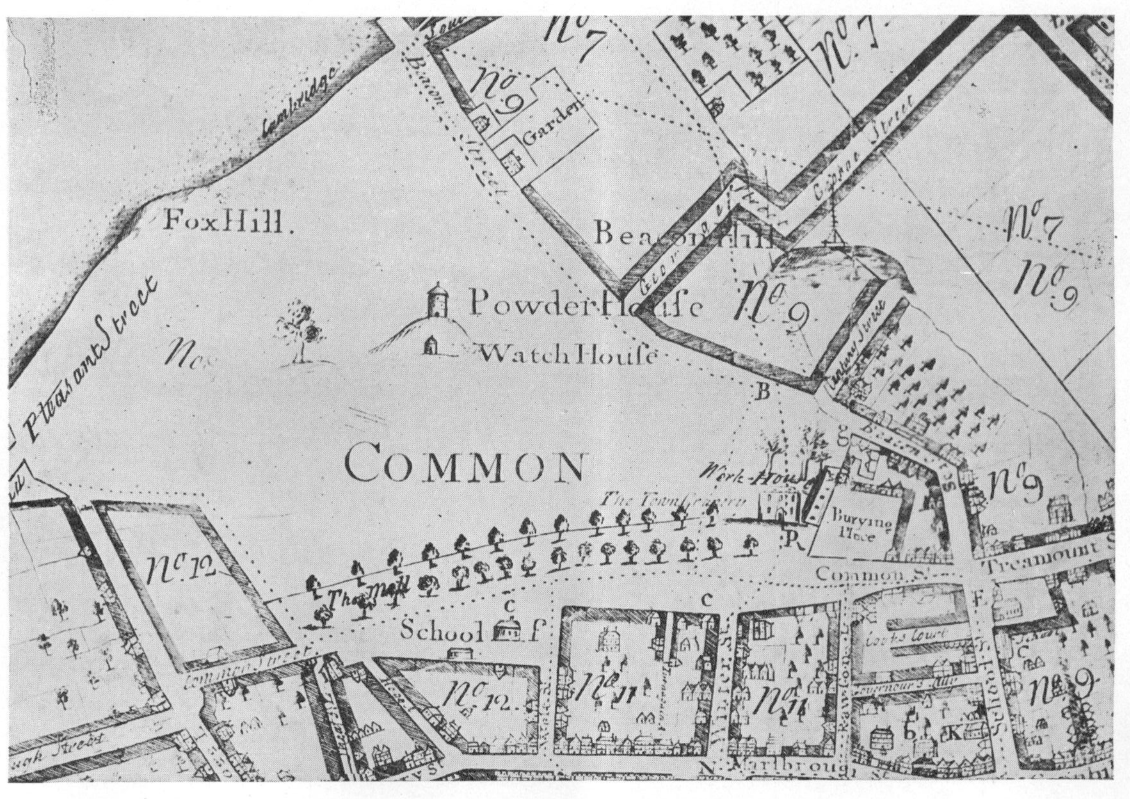

Map of Present Temple Place Section, 1722

Tree. Hastening to the scene he was prevented from removing the figures, but was assured they would be taken down. This was done in the evening and they were burnt on the Common. Hutchinson and the sheriff hearing reports of Oliver's treatment by the mob, wended their way to the latter's house in Milk Street, but were obliged themselves to take safety in flight. These demonstrations, caused by the Stamp Act, were of a different nature when repeated in May, 1766, upon its repeal. Greenleaf, from the windows of his house, saw the erection on the Common of a pyramid, illuminated by 280 lamps. His neighbor, John Hancock, upon the other side of the Common, treated his fellow townsmen to Madeira wine, and the Sons of Liberty set off fireworks in front of the work-house on what is now Park Street and entertained their friends within with refreshments of a liquid nature.

This, however, was but a lull in the storm. In March, 1768, the sheriff again received word that the Liberty Tree had borne fresh fruit and that Paxton and Williams, customs officers, were hanging from the boughs. Before the sheriff's arrival, however, the effigies were removed.

In September, 1766, Greenleaf had assisted the customs officers in their attempt to search the house of Daniel Malcolm, the patriot, on Fleet Street, but they were prevented in their purpose by a great gathering of the people. In June, 1768, the customs officers again met with opposition for seizure of the sloop *Liberty*. This vessel,

Review on the Common, 1768 (After an Old Water Color)

which had lain at the wharf of its owner, John Hancock, for a month and had been used to store oil and tar, was seized, as its contents had not been entered for export. The crowd after handling the officers roughly dragged a boat of the "Collector" up what is now Washington Street to the Liberty Tree opposite Frog Lane (Boylston Street). It was then taken to the Common, where Greenleaf and other onlookers watched it ascend in smoke and flame. News of the affair reached England. Rumors of troops to be sent to the town from the mother country became current. One noon the sheriff, casting his eye across the Common, noticed the beacon on Beacon Hill was prepared to be lighted. Hastily climbing the slope he quietly removed the signal which was to announce the arrival of the troops. They came in September and with bayonets fixed and colors flying, marched to the Common. Barracks were needed for them and the Manufactory House, where Hamilton Place now extends, was selected. It had been leased to Elisha Brown, a weaver, and he objected to vacating. The law was evoked and the sheriff and Hutchinson attempted to get possession. A weaver leaving through a cellar window one noon was pushed aside by Greenleaf who entered and soldiers were posted in the cellar. Brown held the fort in the upper stories, and successfully, for the soldiers were withdrawn in a few weeks.

It was in 1768 that the sheriff was told by Harrison Gray, the province treasurer, as he handed

Boston Common 1799.
after a quaint watercolor drawing of the time. Malcolm Frazer.

Boston Common, 1799 (After _n Old Water Color)

him an execution against Samuel Adams, that he knew his duty and if he failed he would be accountable. But the sheriff as well as his fellow townsmen, patriots and loyalists, were lenient in serving a distress warrant on Adams, in his unfortunate position as tax collector, and amicably settled with him his accounts.

At the trial of the soldiers for the Boston Massacre, Greenleaf performed his official duties as sheriff as he had done previously when Robinson and others were charged with the assault on James Otis. He presented himself at Faneuil Hall while the reports of the tea importers were read and ordered the town's people to disperse. These were all in the line of his official duties, and though after the evacuation of Boston, in April, 1776, his arrest was ordered, like many other loyalists and office-holders under the crown, he was left in possession of his property. In 1765 he had been licensed as an inn-holder and during the siege he had many British officers billeted in his house.

One morning in 1795 Samuel Adams, then governor, who lived just back of Greenleaf on Winter Street, was told that the "old sheriff" was dead. He had died at the ripe age of ninety-one and many recalled the austere but kindly man who had displayed considerable tact during the stormy days before the Revolution.

A granddaughter who lived with him in his declining years married Charles Bulfinch, the architect. The State House on Beacon Hill was one of Bulfinch's buildings. The beginning of its erection the "old sheriff" viewed from the windows of the Usher house.

A French Venture

A daughter of Sheriff Greenleaf married Chief Justice Martin Howard of North Carolina and she with the other executors of her father, sold the house and gardens in 1796. It came into possession of Mrs. Hepsibah (Clark) Swan, wife of James Swan, who was born in Scotland in 1754. He came to Boston as a youth and was employed with Henry Knox in the book shop of Nicholas Bowes in Cornhill. He first came into notice in 1772 by writing a pamphlet against the slave trade. When hostilities commenced after the "Tea Party," of which he was a member, he was an assistant in the treasury office of the province and secretary to the Board of War. He was the companion of Joseph Warren, as a volunteer, at Bunker Hill, but fortunately escaped from the field with the loss of his coat and a broken gun. In May, 1776, he was commissioned a captain in Crafts' Artillery and in November made a major and served in the Continental service. In 1788 he was deputy adjutant general of militia. From 1779 to 1781 he was part owner in the privateer *Boston* and ships *Leighton* and *Prosper* and brigantine *Nancy*. These ventures en-

Charles Bulfinch

Common Street (now Tremont) looking South from West Street, 1800

abled him to purchase the estate of the loyalist Nathaniel Hatch, son of Col. Estes Hatch, in Dorchester. In 1784 Swan bought Burnt Coast Island, Lincoln County, Me. This he paid for with depreciated Continental currency, a shrewd condition inserted in the resolve of the General Court.

The financial conditions of the new republic were unfavorable to Swan's ventures and he left Boston in January 1788. His most pressing creditor was Patrick Jeffries, against whose treatment he expressed himself most bitterly. He went to Havre and Rouen in France, where he investigated French manufactures. On his arrival in France he advanced the interests of the States and in 1790 published in French six letters addressed to Lafayette on the causes of the opposition to commerce between France and the States. In 1790 Swan attempted to negotiate a loan of $2,000,000 for the States from some citizens in Genoa. As an American whose country was a refuge he assisted many royalist refugees to America and also shipped the household effects of others. As many of these people were unfortunate enough to lose their lives, a Boston wit of the last century observed "The guillotine took their heads and Swan took their trunks."

After the horrors of the Revolution, Mrs. Swan joined her husband in his house in the Rue Croix de Petit Champs, and in 1793 he was able to say that he had paid his debts and re-established his ancient fortune and would return,—which he

Common Street (now Tremont), looking North from West Street, about 1800

did in 1794. In the following year he visited Philadelphia with a project to go to Spain in an official capacity.

About this time he became possessed of 25,000 acres in Hardin County, Kentucky, and in 1796 he purchased the Greenleaf estate and placed it in his wife's name and also some lots bought at auction from the town, a part of the site of the future Colonnade Row. At this time his finances again became involved and he sailed in 1797 to France, once more to recoup his fortunes. He was not as successful as during the days of the French Revolution, for ten years later, in 1808, Swan was arrested for a debt due, unjustly as he claimed, to Jean Claud Picquet, a Paris merchant. He was imprisoned for this debt in St. Pelagie prison and stayed there until the Revolution in 1830 opened his prison door. He did not long survive his liberation and died the 18th of March, 1831. Swan's wife had died at their Dorchester house in 1825. Her death invited an attempt by the French creditor to secure payment of Swan's debt to him. The original creditor died before Mrs. Swan and in 1825 his son Anthonie Furcy Picquet came to Boston and applied for letters of administration on the estate of his father who had died in Paris. His property disclosed were 18 Bills of Exchange, drawn by Freytag on James Swan, for 521,646 francs, and accepted by Swan in 1811. This in 1825 with interest amounted to $97,808. The Probate Court not granting administration, Picquet went to the General Court and got a resolve in his favor. The case then went to the Supreme Court and suits were brought in the United States Circuit Court. Meanwhile during the slow course of the law, Picquet became a resident of Boston and acted as the French commercial agent and later as vice-consul. Swan died while the suits were pending. In his will he left a provisional legacy to the city of Boston to be invested in real estate and farms in the vicinity of Boston until a fund of $100,000 was formed. With this an "Orphan Academy" was to be built. But unfortunately for Boston, his estate was insolvent as the Picquet claim was allowed in the courts and debts proved to the amounts of $127,000 and $5,473.34. The Swan assets permitted a payment of but 8.0625 cents on a dollar, and on the 25th of July, 1836, Picquet asked for the amount due to transmit to his brother Cyril Simon, Baron Picquet in Paris. Thus ended the career of the most litigious of the possessors of the Usher house.

Washington Gardens

Swan's own name does not appear in the Boston directory of 1809 as living on Common Street (now Tremont), as he had taken up his enforced residence in St. Pelagie the previous year, but the house and grounds were occupied by the Swan family or remained vacant, till 1813. The next year it was the home of John P. Whitwell. Mr. Whitwell previously resided on Pond Street now Bedford Street. He was an apothecary and

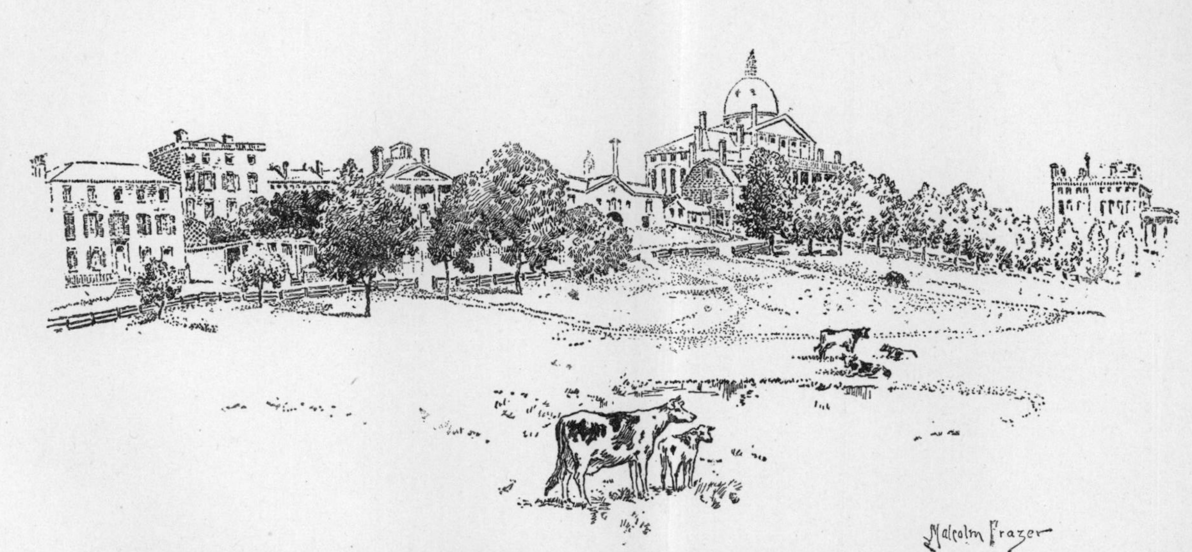

BEACON STREET, FROM THE COMMON, ABOUT 1812

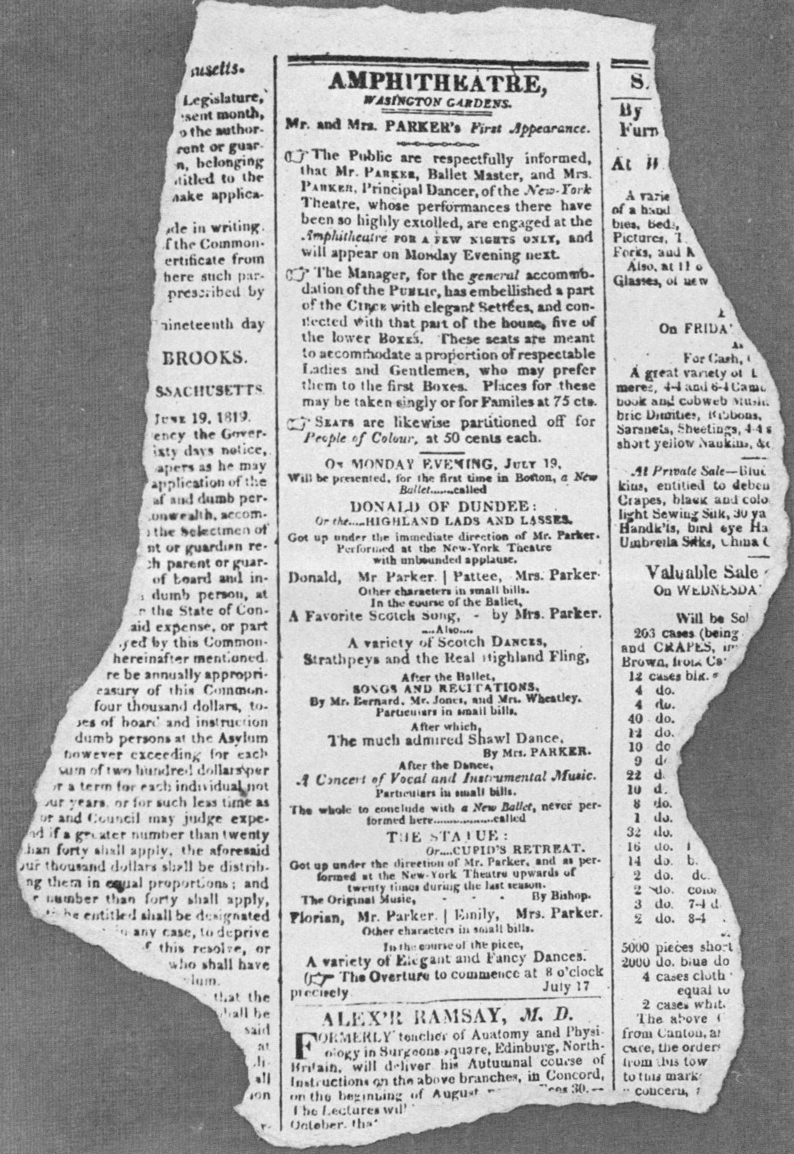

AMPHITHEATRE,

WASINGTON GARDENS.

Mr. and Mrs. PARKER's *First Appearance.*

☞ The Public are respectfully informed, that Mr. PARKER, Ballet Master, and Mrs. PARKER, Principal Dancer, of the *New-York* Theatre, whose performances there have been so highly extolled, are engaged at the *Amphitheatre* FOR A FEW NIGHTS ONLY, and will appear on Monday Evening next.

☞ The Manager, for the *general* accommodation of the PUBLIC, has embellished a part of the CIRCE with elegant Settees, and connected with that part of the house, five of the lower BOXES. These seats are meant to accommodate a proportion of respectable Ladies and Gentlemen, who may prefer them to the first Boxes. Places for these may be taken singly or for Familes at 75 cts.

☞ SEATS are likewise partitioned off for *People of Colour*, at 50 cents each.

ON MONDAY EVENING, JULY 19,
Will be presented, for the first time in Boston, *a New Ballet*......called

DONALD OF DUNDEE:
Or the....HIGHLAND LADS AND LASSES.

Got up under the immediate direction of Mr. Parker.
Performed at the New-York Theatre
with unbounded applause.

Donald, Mr Parker. | Pattee, Mrs. Parker.
Other characters in small bills.
In the course of the Ballet,
A Favorite Scotch Song, - by Mrs. Parker.
....Also....
A variety of Scotch DANCES,
Strathpeys and the Real Highland Fling,

After the Ballet,
SONGS AND RECITATIONS,
By Mr. Bernard, Mr. Jones, and Mrs. Wheatley.
Particulars in small bills.
After which,
The much admired Shawl Dance,
By Mrs. PARKER.
After the Dance,
A Concert of Vocal and Instrumental Music.
Particulars in small bills.

The whole to conclude with *a New Ballet*, never performed here...............called

THE STATUE:
Or....CUPID'S RETREAT.

Got up under the direction of Mr. Parker, and as performed at the New-York Theatre upwards of twenty times during the last season.
The Original Music, - - - By Bishop.
Florian, Mr. Parker. | Emily, Mrs. Parker.
Other characters in small bills.
In the course of the piece,
A variety of Elegant and Fancy Dances.

☞ The Overture to commence at 8 o'clock precisely. July 17

ALEX'R RAMSAY, *M. D.*

FORMERLY teacher of Anatomy and Physiology in Surgeons square, Edinburg, North-Britain, will deliver his Autumnal course of Instructions on the above branches, in Concord, on the beginning of August ... Tees 30.— The Lectures wil... October. tha...

ANNOUNCEMENT OF THE WASHINGTON GARDENS
(From *The Centinel*, July 17, 1819)

his shop was then located at 48 Newbury, now Washington, Street. There one could get Dr. Church's celebrated Cough Drops, likewise his much esteemed Pectoral Pills; and there, also, could be obtained a century ago, June, 1811, for the first time, "Ballstown and Soda Water."

> "The proprietors with much trouble and expense have erected an entire new apparatus by means of which they flatter themselves they have succeeded in preparing a beverage equal in strength and pungency to the boasted soda water of London or New York."

After two years' occupancy, Mr. Whitwell removed his residence to Summer Street.

The next tenant was John H. Schaffer, an auctioneer, who decided to devote the house and grounds to purposes of entertainment. On the 22nd of June, 1815, the "Washington Gardens" were opened. Mr. Hewitt was made the director. Soon after the name of "Vauxhall" was added. One advertisement announced: "the concerts have been monstrously attended and fashionably resorted to and all the arrangements found neat, elegant and orderly, the music excellent."

Later in the summer variegated lamps were hung in the foliage of the garden, and fireworks were displayed. These last were given by David from the Tivoli Gardens, Paris, "the projector of the grand display on the Champ de mars." The summers of 1816 and 1817 saw similar attractions at the "Gardens." In May, 1817, gas lights (which had been introduced in Boston in 1815) were installed there.

On the 9th of December, 1818, William Sullivan, agent of Swan, executed a lease for ten years to Shaffer at an annual rental of $1500 for the house and gardens. Shaffer was also given the privilege to erect any buildings. In 1818 for the first time the theatre seats in the gardens were covered with an awning. In the summer of 1819 Shaffer erected a new brick amphitheatre at a cost of $4,000. The work was done under the supervision of Gridley Bryant, a builder and engineer. Later, in 1824, Bryant designed the United States Bank, with its granite pillars 24 feet long. He was also noted for his inventions. These, however, invited much litigation and he died a poor man.

A typical advertisement of the Washington Gardens at that period was the following:

AMPHITHEATRE

WASHINGTON GARDENS

"The public are respectfully informed that the Amphitheatre will be opened on Friday evening, July 2nd, with an appropriate address under the immediate direction of Mr. Bernard. The entertainments on the first night will consist of recitations, songs and dances. The house will be finished in a style of neatness superior to anything of the kind on this continent. The whole of the scenery, painting and decorations designed and executed by Mr. Worrell. The stage is very handsome and commodious. The circle is floored and provided with settees after the Paris fashion; the boxes will be handsomely fitted up and the whole building properly ventilated. Mr. Bernard, Mrs. Wheatley, and Mr. Batterton of great celebrity from the London theatres will recite and sing. Mr. Jones and others are engaged to form the dances, and in the course of the summer much novelty of talent, and many new pieces will be brought forward with every care, attention and decoration to render them worthy of public patronage."—(*Centinel, 30 June, 1819.*)

The old Usher house was used during the winter season of 1819–20 for the entertainment of parties, societies and the clubs of that period. Wines, liquors and such luxuries as the markets of those days afforded, were advertised. A few gentlemen boarders were accommodated and the stable on the premises gave the same care as the livery stables of the town. The amphitheatre was to be let for any respectable exhibition. In the previous summer there had appeared "Pepin with a company of equestrians and elegant horses after an absence from the metropolis of twelve years."

Amateurs were in evidence in those days as now, and the young men of the Philo-Dramatic Society, of which J. F. Buckingham was president and John Brook treasurer, performed Coleman's "Heir at Law" in July, 1820. At this performance the settees in the front circle were reserved for the Governor and his staff. The Selectmen were also guests on the same occasion. This summer Mr. Brunel had his "philosophical Exhibition, and Enchanted Lady placed in a box disappearing to a nearby pedestal."

Dr. Preston with his exhilarating Nitrous Oxide

Gas appeared in October as the following handbill advertised.

> "Bostonians are charmed with various feats
> At John H. Shaffer's splendid Garden treats,
> Where West is manager and justly draws
> A host of auditors and great applause,
> By showing Yeoman riding upside down,
> Where Godean proved the wonder of the town,
> Where X X X X is retailed by the single glass,
> And Doctor Preston gave his Oxide Gas."

In the summer of 1820, on the estate north of the "Gardens," was erected St. Paul's Church. Shaffer erected in the northwest corner of his Gardens a workshop 40 x 14. This he leased to Solomon Willard, the architect of the church and of Bunker Hill Monument. The next year a similar structure was built 30 x 17 and leased to Henry Ayling, a turner or wood-worker. In August, 1821, Guille made balloon ascensions from the "Gardens," landing with a parachute. It was also in this month, on the eighth, that the West Point Cadets formed a part of the audience. They were encamped on the Common between the Tremont Street Mall and the "Old Elm." On the 11th "on the Ancient military square" on the Common in front of the State House they were presented a stand of colors by the inhabitants.

In June, 1822, appeared a new announcement of the Gardens as the "City Theatre." Mrs. Barrett and Mrs. Reed from the New York Theatre, Miss Turner from New Orleans, and Miss Johnson from New York, appeared during the summer, till September, when the Boston Theatre on Federal Street reopened. The prices were, for the saloon seventy-five cents, boxes fifty cents, and pit twenty-five cents.

In 1825, in honor of Lafayette's visit, his figure was displayed in a transparency placed at the south part of the Gardens. Five large stars also faced to the north. Perhaps among those present some recalled that the owner of the Gardens was still confined in his French prison. A performance this season concluded with "Optical Allusions or Robertson's Phantasmagoria." In those days "Venelli and Lemon, Ice Creams and Fruits" could be obtained during the performances, especially after the fireworks or while witnessing the "Grand Indian War Dance" as performed by a company of Oneida Indians in October, 1828.

During the last few years of Schaffer's lease the amphitheatre was mainly devoted to equestrian performances. In the summer, fireworks were the great attraction. In 1828 there befell to Schaffer the fate of previous owners and tenants and he in turn took part in the drama of the law. In January he had contracted to pay a theatre license of $1,000 and gave bonds for $5,000. He found this a hardship and paid $25 weekly when the theatre was open. During 16 weeks he paid in $400. The city sued him for the balance and won a verdict in the Superior Court. Schaffer appealed to the Supreme Court, where the verdict was affirmed and Schaffer retired from the Gardens

The Masonic Temple, Tremont Street and Temple Place, about 1875

as his lease was soon to expire. He again became an auctioneer and died in a few years.

Freemasonry and the Law

Through a gate about seventy-five feet from the site of St. Paul's Church on Common Street (now Tremont), in 1800, one passed into a lane running just back of the Usher house. This was known as "Turnagain Alley" as there was then no outlet into Newbury, now Washington, Street. An entrance to the Washington Gardens in 1826 from Newbury Street was known as Washington Court. In 1830, just before Swan's death, the estate was cut up into ten lots. Tradition states that the Usher mansion was removed to South Boston and in whole or part became the "Fire Department Hotel" kept by Reed Taft and known later as the "City Point Hotel." The estate contained an acre and forty perches or square rods, nearly fifty-five thousand square feet. A century ago the value of the entire tract was $15,000. At the present time the valuation of this site is from $150 to $200 per square foot, or approximately $9,000,000.

October 14th, 1830, the north corner of the Gardens was the scene of an event important to the Masonic fraternity. The corner stone of the Masonic Temple was laid on that day by Joseph Jenkins, Grand Master of the Grand Lodge

Amos Bronson Alcott

Tremont Street, from Park Street Church, looking South, 1830

of Massachusetts. Mr. Jenkins was a carpenter and builder by trade, and in 1820 had built in New Orleans the Custom House, a great part of the woodwork of which he had prepared in his workshop in Boston and shipped by water.

The erection of the Masonic Temple led to a change of name for Turnagain Alley; it became Temple Court and later Temple Place. For a week, in 1865, it was known as Autumn Street, and in the summer of 1869, for two months, it was called Avon Street.

The exterior of the "Temple" needs no description; it has been pictured in many views during the past seventy-five years. In the basement or first story was a chapel and two school rooms; in the second story a lecture room seating 1,000 persons. In the third story were two halls seating 400 and 200. In the top story was Mason's Hall, a drawing room and rooms accommodating different lodges. The cost of this building of "rubble granite" was about $50,000, including the cost of the land.

This building is of especial interest because it was identified with Emerson and Alcott. In 1834 Amos Bronson Alcott established a school room in 7 Masonic Temple. His first assistant, Elizabeth Peabody, has in her "Record of a School" given the story of the new departure in Boston's

MARGARET FULLER
(MARCHIONESS OSSOLI)

school system by Alcott's educational venture. Later, in 1836, Margaret Fuller (afterwards Marchioness Ossoli) assisted in French and Latin as a teacher.

In 1838 the scholars left abruptly. This re-

Ralph Waldo Emerson

sulted from an incident which indicates the anti-slavery agitation then existing inBoston. Alcott admitted to his school that year a colored girl; this caused the withdrawal of all his pupils, except his own daughters, and the school closed in 1839.

Richard H. Stearns

It was in the Masonic Temple, in 1837, that Emerson gave his course of lectures on history, art, science, literature, politics, and religion. To this famous course, the Lowell Institute Lectures (founded in 1839), succeeded. Later the Swiss Bell Ringers gave their concerts in the Temple.

JUDGE JOHN LOWELL

On October 7th, 1858, the Masonic Temple was sold to the Federal Government for a court house. The court moved from Bowdoin Square, where its sessions had been held for two years in the old Parkman mansion.

Nathan Clifford presided over the Circuit Court.

He was an associate justice of the Supreme Court of the United States. The Federal District Court was presided over by Peleg Sprague, who was succeeded by John Lowell who was appointed by President Lincoln on the 11th of March, 1865.

The old Masonic Temple was destined to experience one more radical change. After its original use for nearly thirty years and the following period of almost thirty years as the seat of the United States Court, the Federal Government in 1885 sold the building at auction. It was bought by the estate of the late William F. Weld, the trustees having already effected plans for remodeling the building and having executed a contract with R. H. Stearns & Company to lease the property if secured. The remodeled building was occupied by the new tenant in the summer of 1886 and continued as their place of business until 1908, when it was completely torn down and the present modern building erected and occupied in the fall of the following year.

The business of R. H. Stearns and Company was founded in 1847 by Richard H. Stearns, who was born in Ashburnham, Mass., December 25, 1824. Soon after his birth, his parents removed to New Ipswich, N. H. Left an orphan at the age of seven, he was taken to Lincoln, Mass., and brought up by his uncle. His education was secured in district schools, and from attending for one year Phillips Academy, Andover, after which for a time he taught school.

He once remarked that he began to earn his

Tremont Street and Temple Place, 1914
(Present store of R. H. Stearns and Company)

own living at the age of seven; meaning, doubtless, that even in childhood he was compelled to make full return in labor upon the farm for board and clothing. His first business experience was selling from house to house on Beacon Hill, a load of potatoes which he had brought from Lincoln to Boston in an ox team.

In 1846 he moved to Boston and found employment in the store of C. C. Burr. A little more than a year later he began business for himself, opening a small store under the old Adams House on Washington Street. This was the obscure beginning of the present successful business, in which the founder took a vital interest until his death in his 85th year. At that time Hon. John D. Long, formerly governor of Massachusetts, who had known and esteemed Mr. Stearns for many years, thus summed up the qualities and achievements of his friend:

> His record as a citizen, public and private, commands universal respect. His private life was such, abounding in charity and good influence so exemplary of the virtues of true citizenship, that it was in itself a public life. I knew him in the legislature of 1875, in social and civic relations, and in his business as a leading merchant of Boston. There was no walk in which his steps were not taken in honor, truth and righteousness.

It is an interesting fact that, although this business has occupied five different buildings during its existence of 67 years, all were located within two and one half blocks of the present store. This stability of location in the retail trade seems to be more marked in Boston than in any other city in the United States. Some years since, when the building of the subway under Tremont Street, and the consequent removal of street cars from the surface was under consideration, Mr. Stearns sought the opinion of a well-known builder as to the probable effect on retail trade in the vicinity, who made this reply: "We cannot move the center of Boston. It was made by the Lord, and fixed for all time."

In these pages there have now been traced some of the changes since the founding of Boston which have occurred on and about the small tract of land which today forms the corner of Tremont Street and Temple Place. From that far-away period when it was bounded by a cow path and when the house of Usher faced on a winding country road from which led "Turnagain Alley," we have come at length to the active business district of a great city, thronged daily by thousands of its own citizens and those of its populous suburbs. If the shadowy forms of Hezekiah Usher and Waitstill Winthrop could rise from the goodly company of Puritans beneath the sod and visit the Boston of today, the headstones in King's Chapel Burying Ground would alone offer a suggestion of their town and time.

State Street in 1804, showing the Union Bank

OLD BOSTON BANKS

And Their Relation to Local and National Development*

Capital tends to accumulate in old and prosperous communities. Early in the history of the North American Colonies, New York, Philadelphia and Boston, because of advantageous location and strong and resourceful citizenship, became the leading communities in population and wealth. Hence these three historic seaboard cities which were indeed the only cities worthy to be so called at the close of the Revolution, became at once the nation's financial centers. This supremacy they have steadily maintained during more than a century of the nation's unparalleled growth. Laboring each in its own way, Boston, New York and Philadelphia together have financed the development of American resources.

Banks and Banking in Old Boston

Each decade in the swift moving industrial life of the republic has brought marked changes, and some of those which have affected or developed the policies of the financial institutions of Boston are of especial interest, as they clearly reflect the progress of state and nation.

Boston may be said always to have been a prosperous community. In early Colonial days

*From information supplied by Francis R. Hart, Vice Chairman of the Board of Directors of the Old Colony Trust Company.

there were, it is true, periods of discouragement but by the close of the Revolution foreign trade had brought success to many Boston merchants. The establishment of banks followed the accumulation of capital. There were two in 1794. The first local institution was the Massachusetts Bank which began business July 5, 1784, with a capital of $300,000, and in 1792 the Union Bank was established. In 1819 there were seven banks in Boston with a capital of $7,300,000; in 1825 nineteen, with a capital of $10,300,000.

The cautious and conservative policies which characterized the management of the early banks, seem to have been impressed upon later generations of bankers and the record of Boston banking makes it plain that those institutions which have earned the confidence of the community have seldom betrayed it. In consequence, each generation of bankers has stood for that which was best in its time, such as the prompt redemption of unreliable currency with a minimum of expense to the holders; the resumption of specie payments, and opposition to all forms of inflation.

In 1847 there were twenty-six banks in Boston (thirteen of which had been chartered at least twenty-five years) with a total capitalization of approximately $21,000,000, and all of which were paying dividends ranging from six to ten per cent. Three years later the number of banks had increased to thirty, having total resources of $42,718,431.

For possibly a little more than a century the

State Street and the Merchants National Bank, 1914

accumulated capital of the citizens of Boston has amounted to an impressive total. Within that period it has found employment in three distinct ways—in local development, in national development and in industrial development. In a broad sense there are also three distinct periods to these investment policies.

Local Uses of Capital

Prior to 1850, no demands were made to finance distant enterprises. Boston, like other cities at that period, was more or less isolated. It was interested in itself and in its near neighbors, but when judged by our present standards, the city had very limited intercourse with other parts of the country. The early citizens of the city were men of clear vision who had faith in their community. In consequence, Boston capital found an outlet in local enterprises. They invested their savings in Boston docks, buildings and bridges. They built highways, reclaimed marshes and cut down Beacon Hill.

The close of the decade from 1840 to 1850, which marked the beginning of the end of Boston's early foreign trade, marked also the close of the period of investment in distinctly local enterprises. New uses for money had begun to appear, especially the railroad, which was to become a factor of supreme importance in the affairs of the city, state and nation, and likewise a mighty consumer of capital. Moreover, though naturally built first in the old settled communities, railroads had even greater reason for existence as arteries to the frontier. Thus it came about that with the resumption of national development after the Civil War, the call came to Boston for financial assistance in distant railway construction. This marked the beginning of the second general policy in connection with the employment of capital.

Railway Building

Unlike the whalers and the clipper ships of an earlier day, of which traditions alone remain, the great railway enterprises which Boston bankers and merchants brought into being during the period from 1850 to 1890 are today a colossal monument to the courage of their promoters. These men supplied the funds which built railroads to the prairie states across the Rocky Mountains through the Northwest, even to the Pacific and into Mexico. It was Boston capital that made possible the Union Pacific, the Atchison, Topeka & Santa Fe, Chicago, Burlington & Quincy, the Oregon railroads, Flint & Pere Marquette, Mexican Central, and many others. With sagacity and vision greater and clearer than even their fathers possessed, the men of Boston laid rails through the wilderness and opened the great West.

Clearly this was a distinct period. Like the education of a son who later becomes strong, the West justified the investment even though profits were not always at once assured. Boston had opened the gates to an empire. Marvelous has

The National Shawmut Bank

been the growth of the enterprises so courageously financed. Yet the appeal of the West to construct railroads was merely the call of a new country for aid. This was obviously a temporary requirement. Struggling roads which at first often terminated at frontier settlements have now become colossal transcontinental systems, no longer requiring the aid or even the counsel of the financial parents.

Meantime the third great use for the accumulated resources of the banks of Boston was fast developing. The new requirement afforded a permanent and normal outlet for a vast aggregate of capital.

Industrial Expansion

A grave situation had been developing in New England. By its activity in constructing railways to the prairies and the Pacific coast, Boston had materially hastened the collapse, for a time at least, of New England agriculture by the competition of the more fertile western prairies. Undismayed, however, New England turned to manufacturing, and with justice demanded the assistance of Boston capital.

From 1850 to 1914 agriculture in the six New England states has in some respects made no progress whatever. Farms are substantially the same in number in 1914 as they were half a century ago. This is equally true of the number of persons employed on them. Cultivated acres have decreased and while the total products of farms have about doubled in value, this is principally due to higher prices. In manufacturing, however, the change has been so extraordinary that it becomes difficult to comprehend. In 1850 there were 183,000 men and 115,000 women employed in all industries in the six New England states, receiving about seventy-two million dollars in wages. Capital invested in manufactures amounted to $160,000,000 and annual products were valued at $275,000,000.

From 1850 to 1910 population in New England increased two and a half times, but the number of persons engaged solely in manufactures quadrupled. They received nearly six hundred millions of dollars in wages. The capital invested amounted to two and a half billions of dollars, and products were valued annually at a little over two and a half billions of dollars.

The magnitude of industrial growth and the changed relationship of capital to value of product suggest the permanent opportunity and duty that came to the bankers of Boston after the great task of financing the railways of the West was approaching completion. It was the call of their own blood. Innumerable new industrial enterprises located in all parts of New England sought for capital. Even more insistent were the well-established enterprises which were entering upon a policy of expansion. Some industrial concerns now represent greater investment than did many of the western railroads at their beginning.

Creation and expansion, however, in a sense

Massachusetts Bank in 1800

First National Bank in 1914
(Successor of the Massachusetts Bank)

would resemble the western railroad situation, and afford but temporary use for capital. There was another more urgent and recurrent use. Upkeep of costly plants, high wages and increased cost of materials together with enormous purchases of raw material demand constantly more capital to conduct prosperous enterprises, and here the comparison between the figures of 1850 and those of 1910 tell the story: In 1850 for each $1000 of capital invested in manufactures in New England, there were products valued at $1,720. In 1910 each dollar invested was merely equivalent to the same amount in value of products. This change of proportion means that if goods could have been produced as cheaply in 1910 as in 1850, the same value of products could have been secured with one billion dollars less capital.

The early uses of Boston capital here traced were obviously a part of the great scheme of development. The third and later use may be considered as the natural and permanent outlet for a generous share of the resources of a great and prosperous community.

The Banks of Boston in 1914

From the two banks of 1794 the number in Boston had increased in 1914 to sixty-two, divided between sixteen national banks, twenty-four trust companies, and twenty-two savings banks. The resources of the national banks has aggregated $372,000,000 and of the trust companies $265,000,000, while deposits in the savings banks amounted to $280,000,000, the total resources of these three classes of Boston banks reaching the huge total of $917,000,000.

Several of the more important banks of Boston were numbered in the group of strong institutions chartered in the first third of the last century, although in some instances consolidation has altered the early names.

The present First National Bank is the successor of the pioneer bank of Boston, the Massachusetts, chartered in 1784. This historic institution was merged with the First National Bank in 1903. In 1847 the capital was $800,000, surplus and deposits $411,000. In 1914 the capital had increased to $5,000,000 and the surplus and deposits to $90,000,000. Something of the city's growth and wealth is suggested by these figures.

FIRST CHARTER SIGNED
JUNE 25, 1792.
BY John Hancock GOV.

The National Union Bank is the oldest of all Boston banks in the sense of unbroken existence under the same name. Established in 1792, it began business in a private residence on State Street. As tenant or owner it has occupied the same site ever since, a continuous residence of one hundred and twenty-two years,—the present building being erected in 1826.

STATE STREET IN 1837
(Old State House in Center and Merchants Bank at the Right)

In 1793, six months after its establishment, the directors declared the first dividend (4 per cent.) and semi-annual dividends have been declared from that date to the present time, without interruption. In this record the bank is unique among American financial institutions. In 1847 its capital was $800,000, and its surplus and deposits were $1,402,194. In 1914 the capital and surplus were $2,000,000 and the total resources $12,723,265.

The Merchants National Bank was established as a state bank in 1831. It occupied the old United States Bank building on State Street and the present Merchants Bank building is located on the same site. In 1847 the total resources were $6,820,000, which had grown in 1914 to the generous figure of $46,000,000.

Largest of all Boston national banks, the Shawmut has attained that position in part through successful management and in part by consolidation. It was established as a state bank in 1837. The paid up capital in 1847 was $500,000, and total resources amounted to $1,212,729.

In 1914 capital and surplus amounted to $15,000,000 and total resources exceeded $116,000,000.

Among the trust companies, a form of banking enterprise which has now become very important, the Old Colony leads in magnitude of resources and influence. This great institution was established in 1890, and in 1914, with two branches and ten distinct departments, it reported resources of over $100,000,000.

This review of the development of banking and investment, especially since 1847, would not be complete without reference to manifestations of the early investment tendencies of the fathers among the Boston financiers of today. Inheritance of property naturally brings with it conservatism. The skill and daring with which the founder of a fortune risked his all and won may not be inherited by his sons and grandsons, and whether it is or not, new conditions and lack of the necessity for aggressive action all result in lessened initiative and increased caution.

Naturally in Boston, which has large inherited wealth, these conditions are plainly observed. Usually they tend to make a community non-progressive, to dishearten the active and ambitious, and to drive such men to more congenial communities, but fortunately for Boston the old aggressive spirit of the pioneer appears in these later generations, as though a racial instinct were manifesting itself. The whalers and the foreign trade have vanished, but the United Fruit Company, a venture in an untried field, was launched by Boston interests and with its fleets and plantations has made a great commercial success.

The researches of a famous Harvard scientist suggested that copper mines offered a vast and profitable field. The Calumet and Hecla and

Court Street Showing Old Colony Trust Company

many other great copper mines developed by Boston capital secured for the city preeminence as the financial center of the copper industry. Boston and New England financed and developed the telephone and later in partnership with New York bore a large part of the burden of establishing all over the United States this colossal and supremely necessary enterprise.

Finally, groups of Boston capitalists have invested great sums of distant industrial or public service development. Working through banking interests, but particularly through enterprises organized and conducted for the purpose, they have aided new cities and states to obtain inter-urban electric railway service and light and power facilities. Stone and Webster, the principal Boston firm in this field, have become nation-wide in their operations. They have been the medium for the investment of more than one hundred and fifty millions of dollars, and have developed inter-urban electric railways and light and power companies, along Puget Sound (in particular about Bellingham and between Everett, Seattle and Tacoma); along the Gulf of Mexico from Houston, Texas, to Pensacola, Florida; elsewhere in Texas; in Nevada, Michigan, Georgia; in many older states in the East and the Middle West, and even as far as Cape Breton and Porto Rico. In all, this firm has organized and started on prosperous careers sixty-seven corporations, each of which is proving of the utmost value and importance to the community it serves. Together they represent a capitalization of more than $186,000,000.

Thus the farsighted policies of old Boston for the application of capital to development still persist. Some of the leaders in advancing these present-day projects are descendants of the old-time merchants who owned the clipper ships of the fifties, or financed the western railways, and so a generous share of the capital and the profits of the Boston of the earlier periods is still at work today aiding at many distant points the national development.

True to the traditional policy of Boston, these chains of widely scattered enterprises have not been mere promotions or schemes of corporate consolidation, but have created public utilities of incalculable importance.

A century and a third have now elapsed since the beginning of the republic. Upon every page of national development appears the evidence of the courage and aid of the three cities with which the United States began her career as a nation. Of these three, Boston, in proportion to population, can claim fairly to have surpassed the others in the great achievement of nation building.